Creative Art & Activities

Puppets

Mary Mayesky

THOMSON
DELMAR LEARNING™

Australia Canada Mexico Singapore Spain United Kingdom United States

Creative Art and Activities: Puppets
Mary Mayesky

Vice President, Career Ed SBU:
Dawn Gerrain

Director of Editorial:
Sherry Gomoll

Acquisitions Editor:
Erin O'Connor

Developmental Editor:
Alexis Ferraro

Editorial Assistant:
Ivy Ip

Director of Production:
Wendy A. Troeger

Production Coordinator:
Nina Tucciarelli

Composition:
Stratford Publishing Services

Director of Marketing:
Donna J. Lewis

Cover Design:
Tom Cicero

Printed in Canada
1 2 3 4 5 XXX 07 06 05 04 03

For more information contact
Delmar Learning,
5 Maxwell Drive,
Clifton Park, NY 12065-2919
at http://www.EarlyChildEd.delmar.com

Library of Congress Cataloging-in-Publication Data

Mayesky, Mary

1-4018-3474-4

NOTICE TO THE READER

To Lucy Mulkeen,

my dear grandaughter,

thank you for the special times we shared with our puppet friends,

Snakey, Priscilla and Milicent.

With love and affection, Grandma Mary

Contents

ACTIVITIES *continued*

Introduction

Welcome to the world of puppets! You will see from the activities in this book that puppets are more than just familiar childhood toys. They are an art form.

Puppets fascinate and involve children in ways few other art forms can, because they allow children to enter the world of fantasy and drama easily. In this magic world, children are free to create whatever they need in their lives.

Traditional puppets, like stick and bag puppets, are found in this book, as are puppets made using such recyclables as paper-towel and toilet-tissue paper rolls, paper plates, paper bags, packaging materials, cardboard and cereal boxes. Once you start making and using these varied puppets, you will be encouraged to create many other unique kinds of puppets from your and the child's imaginations.

The activities in this book are designed for children aged 2 through 8. An icon representing a suggested age for the activity is listed at the top of each activity. However, use your knowledge of the child's abilities to guide you in choosing and using the activities in this book. Wherever appropriate, information is provided on how to adapt the activities for children over age 8.

The focus of this book is a creative approach to making and using puppets in art activities. The activities are meant to be starting points for exploring this art form. Both you and the children are encouraged to explore, experiment, and enjoy the world of puppets.

GETTING STARTED

Process vs. Product

The focus of this book and all early childhood art activities is the process, not the product. This means that the process of creating, not the product, is the main reason for the activity. The joys of creating, exploring materials, and discovering how things look and work are all part of the creative process. How the product looks, what it is "supposed to be," is unimportant to the child, and it should be unimportant to the adult.

Young children delight in the experience, the exploration, and the experimentation of art activities. The adult's role is to provide interesting materials and an environment that encourages children's creativity. Stand back when you are tempted to "help" children working with puppets. Instead, encourage all children to discover their own unique abilities.

Using Puppets

Puppets are usually first used in nursery or preschool, where they are invaluable. Puppets can teach finger plays; hand puppets can act out familiar nursery rhymes. The shy child who is reluctant to sing often will participate through a puppet. Puppetry is a sure means of stimulating creative storytelling in young children.

Puppets offer children two experiences: (1) the creative experience of making puppets and (2) the imaginative experience of making puppets come to life.

Considering the Child

Young children find it hard to wait patiently to use materials in an activity. Often, the excitement of creativity and patience do not mix. In addition, it is sometimes difficult for young children to share. With young children, plan to have enough materials for each child. For example, having enough fabric scraps for each child to dress a puppet makes the activity more fun and relaxed for young children.

Gathering Materials

Each activity in this book includes a list of required materials. It is important to gather all materials before starting an activity with children. Children's creative experiences are easily discouraged when children must sit and wait while the adult looks for the tape, extra scissors, or colored paper. Be sure to gather materials in a place the children can easily access.

Storing and Making Materials Available

Having the materials to make puppets is not enough. These materials must be stored and readily accessible to the children. For example, scraps of materials and trim bunched in a paper bag discourages children from using them. Storing such materials in a clear plastic box that is shallow enough for children to easily search works much better. Storing buttons in a recycled muffin tin or even in a fishing box with lots of compartments keeps these supplies orderly and encourages their use. Many teachers find clear-plastic shoeboxes invaluable for storing all the "fancy" materials children use to decorate their puppet creations. Such boxes, great for storing and stacking all kinds of art materials, are available at economy stores. **Figure 1** gives some added hints for storing materials for puppet making and other creative activities.

Be creative when thinking about storing and making materials available for your little puppet masters. Storing supplies in handy boxes and other containers makes creating puppets and cleaning up after puppet making more fun.

Using Food Products

Several activities involve the use of different kinds of foods. There are long-standing arguments for and against food use in art activities. For example, many teachers have long used potato printing as a traditional printing activity for young children. These teachers feel potatoes are an economical way to prepare printing objects for children. Using potatoes beyond their shelf life is an alternative to throwing them away. On the other hand, many teachers feel that food is for eating and should be used for nothing else.

This book has many activities that do not use food so that there will be options for teachers who oppose food use in art activities. Also, where possible, alternatives to food items are suggested. Whatever your opinion, creative puppet activities are provided for your and the children's exploration and enjoyment.

Employing Safe Materials

For all activities in this book and for any art activities for young children, be sure to use safe art supplies. Read labels on all art materials. Check materials for age appropriateness. The Art and Creative Materials Institute (ACMI) labels art materials AP (approved

FIGURE 1 · TIPS FOR STORING ART MATERIALS

The ways materials, supplies, and space are arranged can make or break children's and teachers' art experiences. Following are suggestions for arranging supplies for art experiences:

1. *Scissor holders*. Holders can be made from gallon milk or bleach containers. Simply punch holes in the containers and place scissors in the holes with the scissor points to the inside. Egg cartons turned upside down with slits in each mound also make excellent holders.
2. *Paint containers*. Containers can range from muffin tins and plastic egg cartons to plastic soft-drink cartons with baby food jars in them. These work especially well outdoors as well as indoors, because they are large and not easily tipped. Place one brush in each container. This prevents colors from mixing and makes cleanup easier.
3. *Crayon containers*. Juice and vegetable cans painted or covered with contact paper work very well.
4. Crayon pieces may be melted in muffin trays in a warm oven. These pieces, when cooled, are nice for rubbings or drawings. Crayola® makes a unit that is designed specifically for melting crayons safely.
5. Printing with tempera is easier if the tray is lined with a sponge or a paper towel.
6. A card file for art activities helps organize the program.
7. *Clay containers*. Airtight coffee cans and plastic food containers are excellent ways to keep clay moist and always ready for use.
8. *Paper scrap boxes*. By keeping two or more boxes of scrap paper of different sizes, children will be able to choose the size paper they want more easily.
9. Cover a wall area with pegboard and suspend heavy shopping bags or transparent plastic bags from hooks inserted in the pegboard to hold miscellaneous art supplies. Hang smocks in the same way on the pegboard (at child level, of course).
10. Use the back of a piano or bookcase to hang a shoe bag. Its pockets can hold many small items.
11. Use divided frozen food trays or a revolving lazy Susan to hold miscellaneous small items.

(From Mayesky, Mary. *Creative Activites for Young Children*, 7th ed., Clifton Park, NY: Delmar Learning.)

product) and CL (certified label). Products with these labels are certified safe for use by young children.

The ACMI provides an extensive list of materials and manufacturers of safe materials for all young children. This information is available on the ACMI Web site at http://www.acminet.org or by writing to 715 Boylston Street, Boston, MA 02116.

Some basic safety hints for art activities are:

- Always use products that are appropriate for the child. Use nontoxic materials for children in Grades 6 and lower.
- Never use products for skin painting or food preparation unless the products are intended for those uses.
- Do not transfer art materials to other containers. You will lose the valuable safety information on the product packages.
- Do not eat or drink while using art and craft materials. Wash after use. Clean yourself and your supplies.
- Be sure that your work area is well ventilated.

Potentially unsafe art supplies for puppet making include:

- *Powdered clay.* Powdered clay is easily inhaled and contains silica, which harms the lungs. Instead, use wet clay, which cannot be inhaled.
- *Instant papier-mâché.* Instant Papier-mâché may contain lead or asbestos. Use only black-and-white newspaper and wheat paste or liquid starch.
- *Epoxy, instant glues, or other solvent-based glues.* Use only water-based, white glue.
- *Paints that require solvents like turpentine to clean.* Use only water-based paints.
- *Cold water or commercial dyes that contain chemical additives.* Use only natural vegetable dyes made from beets, onion skins, and so on.
- *Permanent markers.* Permanent markers may contain toxic solvents. Use only water-based markers.

Be aware of all children's allergies. Children with allergies to wheat, for example, may be irritated by the wheat paste used in papier-mâché . Other art materials that may cause allergic reactions include chalk or other dusty substances, water-based clay, and any material that contains petroleum products.

Also be aware of children's habits. Some young children put everything in their mouths. (This can be the case at any age.) Others may be shy and slow to accept new materials. Use your knowledge of children's tendencies to help you plan art activities that are safe for all children.

Creating a Child-Friendly Environment

It is difficult to be creative when you have to worry about keeping yourself and your work area clean. Remember to cover the children. Some good coverups are men's shirts (with the sleeves cut off), aprons, pillowcases with holes cut for the head and arms, and smocks. Some fun alternatives are sets of old clothes or shoes that can be worn as "art clothes." These old clothes could become "art journals" as they became covered with the traces of various art projects.

Creating a Child's Art Environment

Encourage young artists by displaying appropriate art prints and other works of art. Do not make the mistake of thinking young children do not enjoy "grownup art." Children are never too young to enjoy the colors, lines, patterns, and designs of artists' work. Art posters from a local museum, for example, can brighten an art area. Such posters also get children looking at and talking about art, which encourages the children's creative work.

Display pieces of pottery, shells and rocks, and other beautiful objects from nature to encourage children's appreciation of the lines, symmetries, and colors of nature. Even the youngest child can enjoy the look and feel of smooth, colored rocks or the colors of fall leaves. All these are natural parts of a child's world that can be talked about with young children as those children create artwork. Beautiful objects encourage creativity.

Starting to Collect

The more exciting "extras" you can collect, the more fun the puppet activities in this book will be for the children. You cannot start too soon collecting materials for these activities. You can probably add items to the following list, which suggests some puppet materials. Ask friends and parents to collect some of these materials, too.

Paper scraps
Fabric scraps
Wallpaper scraps
Rickrack and other sewing trims
Buttons
Pompoms
Sequins
Feathers
Popsicle/craft sticks
Paper bags
Paper plates
Styrofoam and paper cups
Boxes of varied sizes
Yarn and ribbon scraps
Straws

Enter the world of puppets in the pages that follow. Enjoy the trip!

Balloon Puppets

MATERIALS

- ☐ balloons
- ☐ markers
- ☐ glue
- ☐ pieces of yarn and trim
- ☐ masking tape

HELPFUL HINTS

- These puppets are not made to last. Be prepared for a lot of popping fun as children create their balloon puppets.
- Have extra balloons on hand for children who work fast. They may want to make two or three.

DEVELOPMENTAL GOALS

Develop creativity, small muscles in hands and fingers, and hand-eye coordination and use familiar objects in new ways.

PREPARATION

You can blow up the balloons—one for each child—or, if the children are able, let them blow up the balloons. Some children will need some assistance. Tie the ends of the balloons. Talk about how to handle the balloons so they will not break. Have extras on hand in case they do break.

PROCESS

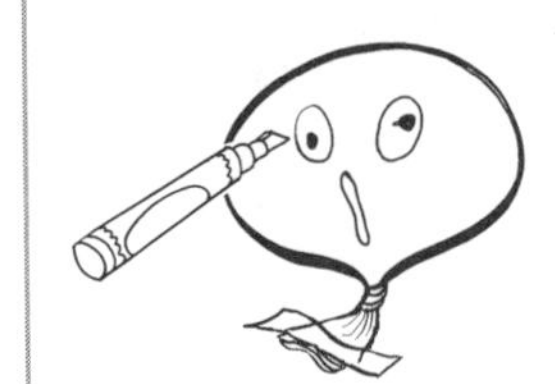

1. Tape the balloon to the table.
2. Use markers to make a face on the balloon.
3. Glue yarn on top for hair.
4. Add other pieces of fabric for clothing.
5. Untape the balloon when finished decorating it and enjoy!

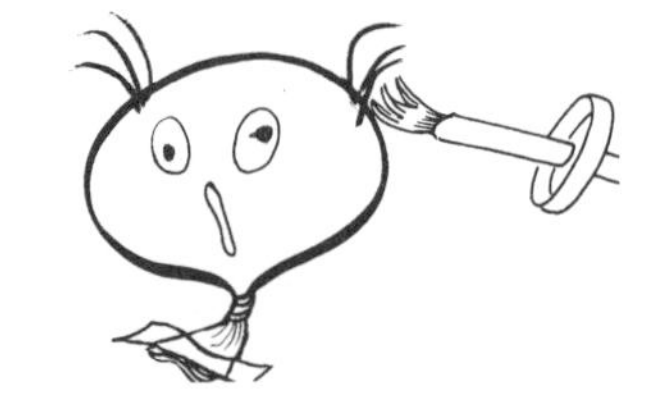

VARIATIONS

- Never use balloons with children 3 and younger.
- Use balloons of different shapes to create fanciful animals.
- Make a balloon body with other balloons taped to the head.

NOTES FOR NEXT TIME: ____

____

____

____

____

Basic Hand Puppets

MATERIALS

- ☐ scraps of fabric, felt pieces, yarn, and trim
- ☐ glue
- ☐ needle and thread (optional)
- ☐ scissors

HELPFUL HINTS

- Older children enjoy sewing the puppets together themselves. Rug needles that have large eyes and somewhat blunt tips work well for this age group.
- You may have to help the child sew or staple the two puppet pieces together.
- Many fabric glues stick the two puppet pieces together very well.

DEVELOPMENTAL GOALS

Develop creativity and small muscles in hands and fingers; use familiar objects in new ways; and learn the design concepts of detail placement, color, and pattern.

PREPARATION

Use the child-sized hand pattern on the next page to cut out two hand-puppet pieces for each child.

PROCESS

1. Give each child two hand-puppet pattern pieces: one for the front of the puppet and one for the back.
2. Glue on bits of felt for facial features.
3. Glue on yarn for hair, in the front and back, if desired.
4. Sew or glue the two puppet pieces together.
5. When using glue, let the glue dry well before using the puppet.

VARIATIONS

- Staple the puppets together.
- Use buttons, odd bits of jewelry, and sequins for decorative details for children 4 and older.

NOTES FOR NEXT TIME: ____________________

____

____

____

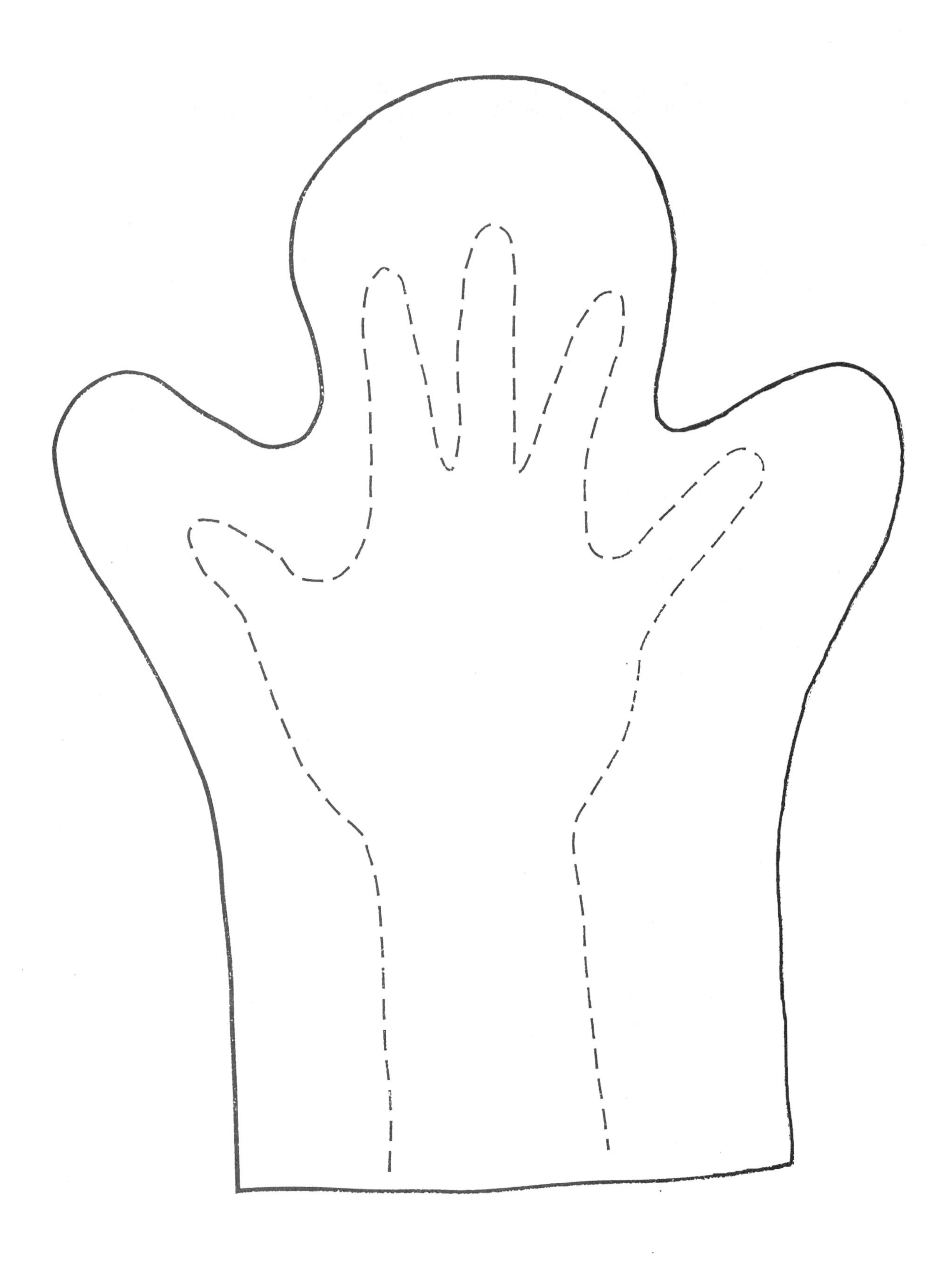

Basic Stick Puppets

MATERIALS

- ☐ all types of sticks (e.g., large twigs, Popsicle sticks, small pieces of smooth lumber)
- ☐ pieces of cloth
- ☐ cotton balls
- ☐ newspaper
- ☐ rubber bands or strings

HELPFUL HINTS

- Scrap yarn, wood shavings, and buttons are good materials for decorating the puppet's face.
- Using the stick, move the puppet side to side, up and down, or in any direction.

DEVELOPMENTAL GOALS

Develop creativity, small motor skills, and hand-eye coordination and encourage imagination.

PREPARATION

If using newspaper to stuff the puppet's head, wad the newspaper into small balls. Let the children help you do this—They love it!

PROCESS

1. Place a piece of cloth over the stick.
2. Stuff the cloth with wads of newspaper or cotton balls.
3. Attach the stuffed cloth to the stick with a piece of string or a rubber band, making a head.
4. Consider using a rubber band instead of string to form the head.

VARIATIONS

- Decorate the head with crayons or colored paper and paste.
- Use scrap pieces of fabric or wallpaper to dress the puppet.

NOTES FOR NEXT TIME: ______________________________

____

____

____

Box Puppets

MATERIALS

- ☐ small boxes (from pudding or gelatin)
- ☐ construction paper
- ☐ paste
- ☐ scissors
- ☐ scrap pieces of fabric and trim
- ☐ masking tape
- ☐ markers
- ☐ crayons

HELPFUL HINTS

- For some young artists, it may be better not to try to cover the box with construction paper. Instead, they may enjoy coloring directly onto the box.
- Covering boxes with construction paper to make box puppets is appropriate for children with well-developed small muscle skills.

DEVELOPMENTAL GOALS

Develop creativity, small muscles in hands and fingers, and hand-eye coordination; use familiar objects in new ways; and learn the design concepts of detail placement, color, and pattern.

PREPARATION

Give each child two small boxes.

PROCESS

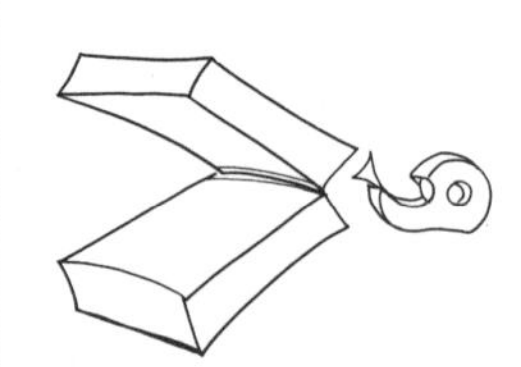

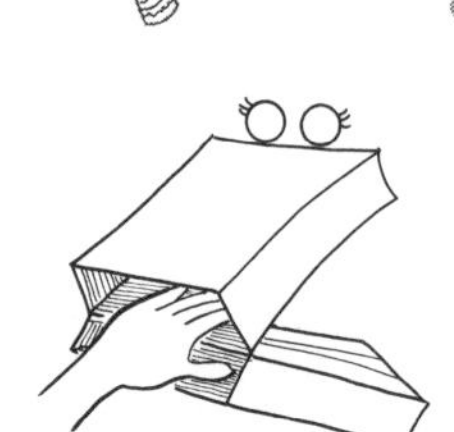

1. Tape the two boxes together, keeping the openings on both free.
2. Cover the boxes with construction paper.
3. The top box is the eye and top of the mouth.
4. The bottom box is the bottom part of the mouth
5. Add bits of colored paper for eyes, a mouth, and other details.
6. Add ears on the side of the boxes, if desired.
7. When all adhesives are dry, use and enjoy the puppet.
8. To use the puppet, place four fingers in the top box and the thumb in the bottom box to work the mouth.

VARIATIONS

- Use large boxes for big puppets. Be sure, however, that the boxes are small enough for little hands.
- Have fun making big tongues on the bottom box that will wag when the puppet talks.
- Add yarn hair that will be floppy and fun when the puppet moves.

NOTES FOR NEXT TIME: ______________________________

Bristle-Brush Puppets

MATERIALS

- ☐ wool sock or tube sock
- ☐ bristle brush
- ☐ buttons
- ☐ thumbtacks
- ☐ string
- ☐ glue

HELPFUL HINT

- This activity is appropriate for children 5 years and older.

DEVELOPMENTAL GOALS

Develop creativity, small muscles in hands and fingers, and hand-eye coordination; use familiar objects in new ways; and appreciate recycling.

PREPARATION

An adult should be available to help push thumbtacks through the sock and into the brush. The thumbtack is pushed from the inside of the sock into the base of the brush to attach the brush to the sock.

PROCESS

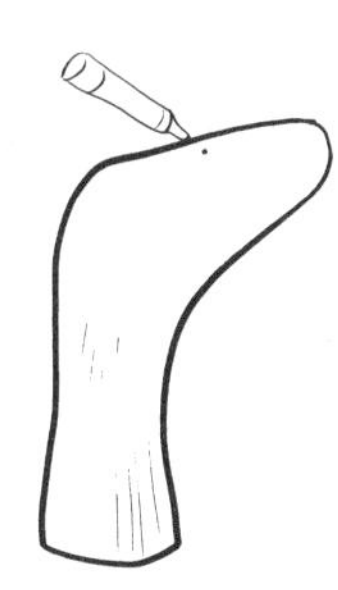

1. Try the sock on a hand to determine where the head will be.
2. Mark this spot.
3. Use thumbtacks to attach the brush to this spot.The brush becomes the puppet's hair.
4. Glue pieces of string to the sock for whiskers.
5. Glue buttons to the sock for eyes.
6. Tie a piece of string around the sock to make the puppet's neck.

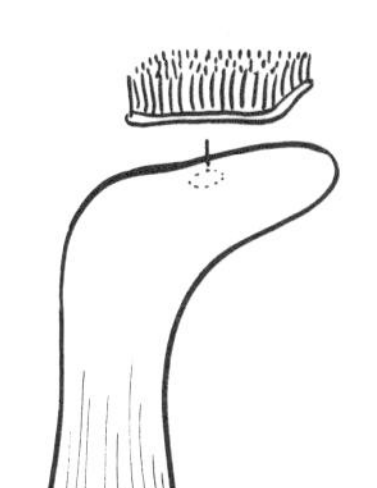

VARIATIONS

- Use colored markers to add texture details to the sock.
- Make bristle puppets out of socks of varied sizes and colors.
- Glue on "wiggly" eyes.
- Use different sizes and shapes of brushes for the bristle tops.

NOTES FOR NEXT TIME: ______________________________

____

____

____

Coat-Hanger Puppets

MATERIALS

- ☐ wire coat hangers
- ☐ old nylon stockings or pantyhose
- ☐ cloth tape
- ☐ yarn
- ☐ felt scraps
- ☐ buttons
- ☐ scissors
- ☐ glue

HELPFUL HINTS

- When using pantyhose, cut off the legs so they can be used separately.
- Some children may be able to stretch the hose over the hanger. Let them try.
- An adult must do the bending and taping of the hanger's hook.

DEVELOPMENTAL GOALS

Develop creativity, small muscles in hands and fingers, and hand-eye coordination and learn the design concepts of pattern, detail placement, and symmetry.

PREPARATION

Stretch the hanger into a diamond shape. Pull the stocking over it and tie at the bottom. Bend the hook into an oval and tape it in place so it will not poke the children.

PROCESS

1. Decorate the puppet by gluing on felt scraps for facial features.
2. Glue on yarn for hair, if desired.
3. Use buttons for eyes.
4. Work the puppet with the tape-covered oval as a handle.

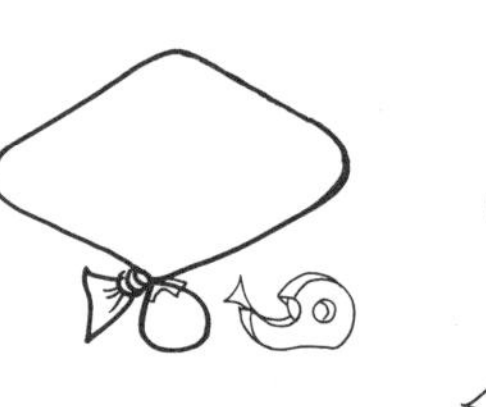

VARIATIONS

- Make an original creation that does not have to be a person.
- Give the puppet a name and act out a story with it.
- Use different colors of hose for variety.

NOTES FOR NEXT TIME: ______________________________

Cone Finger Puppets

MATERIALS

- ☐ thread cones
- ☐ glue
- ☐ scraps of fabric, felt, trim, and yarn
- ☐ buttons
- ☐ scissors
- ☐ construction paper
- ☐ crayons
- ☐ markers

HELPFUL HINT

- Tailor shops and dry-cleaning stores are good sources of thread cones.

DEVELOPMENTAL GOALS

Develop creativity, small muscles in fingers and hands, and hand-eye coordination and learn the design concepts of color, details, and pattern.

PREPARATION

Talk about the shape of the cone. Discuss what kind of puppet it would make. Talk about such details as face, body shape, and clothing type. Talk about what kind of animal it would make, too.

PROCESS

1. Cut a head from construction paper.
2. Add details with crayons and markers.
3. Glue head to the top of the cone.
4. Add fabric scraps to the cone for clothing.
5. Glue on construction paper arms, if desired.

VARIATIONS

- If thread cones are hard to find, make the cones out of paper or felt.
- Use a ping-pong ball for the head. Cut a hole in the bottom of the ping-pong ball and glue it to the top of the cone.
- Make cone finger puppets from another planet. Let the puppet talk about what it is like on his planet.
- Make cone finger puppets for story characters. Let the children guess which ones they are.

NOTES FOR NEXT TIME: ______________________________

Cutout-Figure Stick Puppets

MATERIALS

- ☐ construction paper
- ☐ markers
- ☐ crayons
- ☐ paste
- ☐ Popsicle or craft sticks
- ☐ scraps of fabric and trim
- ☐ buttons
- ☐ sequins
- ☐ beads
- ☐ scissors

HELPFUL HINTS

- Very young children will need help cutting out the figures.
- Let children who can cut well help other children cut out their figures.
- Do not use beads and sequins for children under 3 years old.

DEVELOPMENTAL GOALS

Develop creative thinking, small motor skills, and hand-eye coordination and reinforce the idea of recycling.

PREPARATION

Give each child a piece of construction paper. Talk about the kinds of puppet the children might like to make. Talk about favorite people in the children's lives, familiar story book or nursery rhyme characters, and so on.

PROCESS

1. Draw a figure on the construction paper.
2. Cut out the figure.
3. Paste the figure onto a Popsicle stick.
4. After the paste dries, decorate the figure.
5. Use pieces of fabric and trim to dress the stick figure.
6. Use beads and sequins as features and decorations.

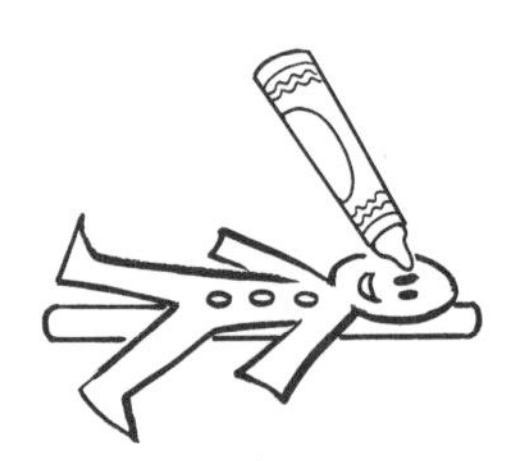

VARIATIONS

- Cut pictures from magazines or old picture books. Glue the pictures to construction paper and cut them out, then glue them to sticks and decorate.
- Use old photographs for this activity. Cut out photos and glue them to sticks.

NOTES FOR NEXT TIME: ______________________________

____

____

____

Cut-Up Puppets

MATERIALS

- ☐ damaged or outdated children's books
- ☐ Popsicle or craft sticks
- ☐ paste
- ☐ scissors

- Cut-up puppets make good use of damaged children's books.
- Let the children tell stories using the cut-out puppets.

DEVELOPMENTAL GOALS

Develop creativity and small muscles in hands and fingers and encourage recycling and dramatic play.

PREPARATION

Collect used and damaged children's books from garage or rummage sales.

PROCESS

1. Go through a book to choose pictures of people or animals.
2. Cut out the pictures.
3. Paste the pictures to a Popsicle stick.
4. Use the puppets to tell a story.

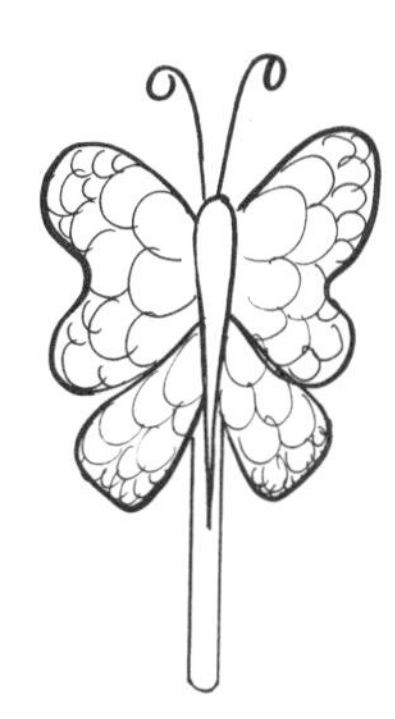

VARIATION

- Glue pictures of cartoon characters from advertisements to construction paper. Cut out and paste the pictures to Popsicle sticks to use as puppets.

NOTES FOR NEXT TIME: ____________________

____

____

____

Cylinder Puppets

MATERIALS

- ☐ pieces of 4-1/2" × 12" drawing or construction paper
- ☐ stapler and staples (or glue)
- ☐ yarn
- ☐ scraps of fabric and ribbon

HELPFUL HINTS

- Be sure the cylinder fits over two of the child's fingers before stapling or gluing the cylinder closed.
- For very young children, make the cylinder fit over four of the child's fingers.

DEVELOPMENTAL GOALS

Develop creativity and small muscles in hands and fingers; understand design concepts of color, shape, and detail concepts; and encourage imagination.

PREPARATION

Give each child a piece of drawing or construction paper pre-cut to size indicated in list of materials.

PROCESS

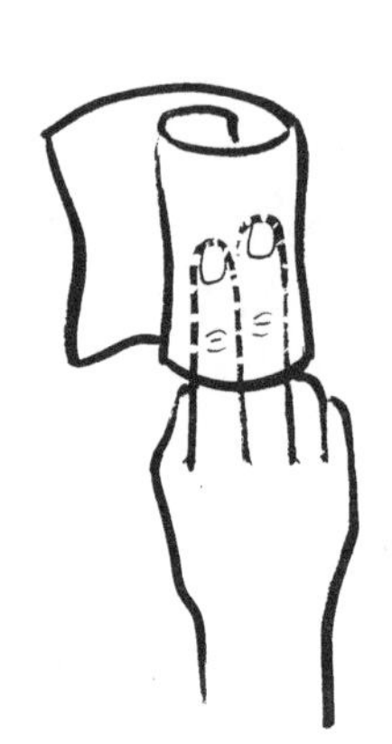

1. Roll the paper into a cylinder that fits over two of the child's fingers.
2. Staple or glue the cylinder together. This is the head of the puppet.
3. Using paper, scissors, and paste, make a face on the tube.
4. Use paper, yarn, and scrap bows to decorate the puppet.
5. Slip the puppet over two of the child's finger to use.

VARIATIONS

- Cut out a body, skirt, or suit and paste or staple it to the tube.
- Make real or imaginary animal cylinder puppets.

NOTES FOR NEXT TIME: ______________________________

____

____

____

Detergent-Bottle Puppet Racks

MATERIALS

- ☐ small, plastic detergent bottles
- ☐ bolts
- ☐ scraps of lumber or drywall

- Puppet racks are nice places for puppets to "rest." They are much nicer and more attractive than puppet piles!

DEVELOPMENTAL GOALS

Use familiar objects in new ways and develop sense of order.

PREPARATION

Wash and dry the plastic bottle. Keep the cap on the bottle.

PROCESS

1. Make a hole in the bottom of the plastic bottle.
2. Screw the bolt into the piece of lumber or drywall from the bottom up.
3. Keep screwing the bolt until it penetrates the top of the drywall or lumber.
4. Place the plastic bottle on top of the bolt.
5. Continue screwing the bolt until the plastic bottle is secured on the drywall or lumber.
6. Place a puppet over the detergent bottle for convenient storage.

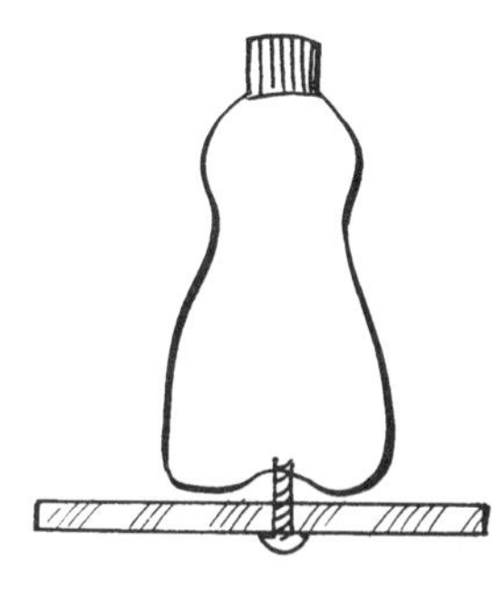

VARIATIONS

- When drywall and lumber pieces are unavailable, use heavy cardboard.
- Any plastic bottles the size of detergent bottles work well as puppet racks.

NOTES FOR NEXT TIME: ______________________________

Envelope Puppets

MATERIALS

- ☐ white envelopes
- ☐ markers
- ☐ scissors
- ☐ crayons

- Envelope puppets are appropriate for even very young children because they are easy to make and use. You may have to help young children cut off the bottom edges of the envelopes, however.

DEVELOPMENTAL GOALS

Develop creativity, small muscles in fingers and hands, and hand-eye coordination and use familiar objects in new ways.

PREPARATION

Give each child a white envelope.

PROCESS

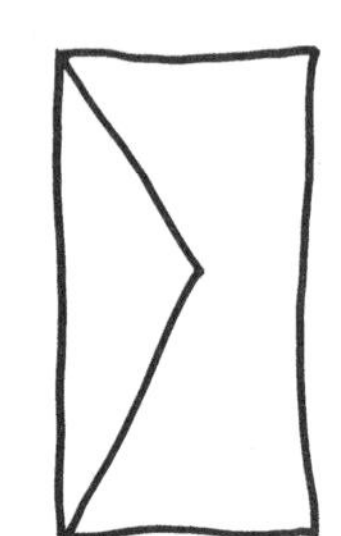

1. Seal the envelope.
2. Draw a face on the envelope lengthwise.
3. Add facial details with markers and crayons.
4. Cut off the bottom edge of the envelope.
5. Slip the puppet on the hand and use as a puppet.

VARIATIONS

- Glue on yarn for hair, buttons for eyes, and any other decorative effect desired.
- Make envelope animals and act out "Farmer in the Dell."
- Make a family of envelope puppets for the housekeeping corner.

NOTES FOR NEXT TIME: ______________________________

____

____

____

Feeling Puppets

MATERIALS

- ☐ paper plates
- ☐ Popsicle or craft sticks
- ☐ glue
- ☐ stapler and staples
- ☐ crayons
- ☐ markers
- ☐ scraps of yarn, fabric, and trim

HELPFUL HINT

- Shy children often find that puppets help them express their feelings.

DEVELOPMENTAL GOALS

Develop creativity, small muscles in fingers and hands, and hand-eye coordination and encourage feelings of expression.

PREPARATION

Talk about feelings. Ask the children to define words like *happy*, *sad*, *moody*, and *troubled*.

PROCESS

1. Give each child a paper plate.
2. Have the child choose an emotion to show on the paper-plate face.
3. Draw a face on the plate depicting the chosen emotion.
4. Add such details as yarn hair and button earrings.
5. Glue or staple a stick to the bottom of the plate.
6. Have the child use the puppet to explain what the puppet is feeling and why.

VARIATIONS

- From a group of feeling puppets, let the child choose a puppet and explain the puppet's feeling.
- Have each child make a happy and a sad puppet. Let the children express their feelings by choosing the corresponding puppet.

NOTES FOR NEXT TIME: ______________________________

____

____

____

Finger-Leg Puppets

MATERIALS

- ☐ construction paper
- ☐ markers
- ☐ crayons
- ☐ buttons
- ☐ scraps of fabric and trim
- ☐ glue
- ☐ stapler and staples

HELPFUL HINT

- When making this type of puppet the first time, a sample may help the children, but try not to display the sample because doing so discourages creativity. Encourage the children to create their own finger-leg puppets.

DEVELOPMENTAL GOALS

Develop creativity, small muscles in hands and fingers, and hand-eye coordination and encourage imagination.

PREPARATION

Cut construction paper in strips 1-inch wide and wide enough to encircle the child's index and middle fingers.

PROCESS

1. Measure a construction paper strip around the child's index and middle fingers.
2. Glue or staple the strip so it forms a ring.
3. Draw and cut out the top part of a figure. Do not draw legs.
4. Glue or staple the figure to the paper ring.
5. Slip the puppet over the child's index and middle fingers. The child's fingers are the puppet's legs.

VARIATIONS

- Make animal finger-leg puppets.
- Do finger plays using finger-leg puppets.

NOTES FOR NEXT TIME: ______________________________

____

____

____

Finger-Cap Puppets

MATERIALS

- ☐ construction paper
- ☐ crayons
- ☐ markers
- ☐ scraps of fabric and trim
- ☐ glue
- ☐ buttons
- ☐ any other decorative items
- ☐ stapler and staples

HELPFUL HINTS

- Finger-cap puppets are great for all children, even toddlers, because they are easy to use. However, do not use buttons with toddlers and children under 3.
- Have older children measure each other for finger rings.

DEVELOPMENTAL GOALS

Develop creativity, small muscles in fingers and hands, and hand-eye coordination and encourage imagination.

PREPARATION

Cut 1-inch-wide strips of construction paper the length of the child's index finger.

PROCESS

1. Measure a 1-inch strip of construction paper around the child's index finger.
2. Glue or staple the strip so it forms a ring.
3. Draw a face on construction paper.
4. Decorate the face with yarn hair, buttons for eyes, and so on.
5. Glue the face to the construction-paper ring.
6. When the glue is dry, slip the ring over the child's index finger for play.

VARIATIONS

- Make a finger-cap puppet for each finger. Have a singalong using the finger-cap puppets as a chorus.
- Hold a performance with one child as the entire cast.
- Do fingerplays using the finger-cap puppets to act it out.

NOTES FOR NEXT TIME: ______________________________

____

____

____

Finger-Face Puppets

MATERIALS

- ☐ felt-tip markers

HELPFUL HINTS

- Finger-face puppets are very easy to manipulate, even by toddlers.
- Finger puppets encourage small-muscle action, which is great for developing small motor control in the hands and fingers.
- Finger-face puppets are the least expensive, easiest puppets to make. Therefore, there is no excuse for excluding them from the young child's world.
- Ensure that parents approve of children drawing on their fingers.

DEVELOPMENTAL GOALS

Develop creativity, hand-eye coordination, and small muscles in hands and fingers and encourage imagination.

PREPARATION

Give each child a felt-tip pen.

PROCESS

1. Draw a face on the index finger with the felt-tip pen.
2. Draw faces on the four remaining fingers and the thumb, too.
3. The child's fingers become the puppets' faces.

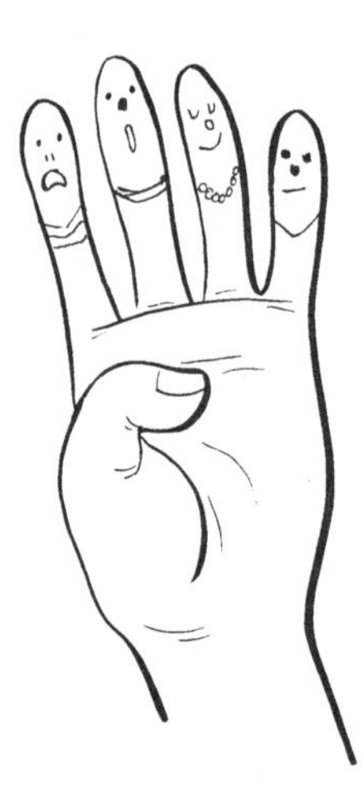

VARIATIONS

- Let the children draw faces on each others' fingers.
- Do fingerplays with the finger-face puppets.
- Have one child perform a show as the entire cast.

NOTES FOR NEXT TIME: ____________________

Foam-Tray Puppets

MATERIALS

- ☐ markers
- ☐ glue
- ☐ construction paper
- ☐ craft sticks
- ☐ recycled foam produce trays
- ☐ scraps of fabric and trim
- ☐ yarn and ribbon scraps
- ☐ buttons
- ☐ sequins
- ☐ scissors

HELPFUL HINTS

- Ask parents to save foam trays for this and other art activities.
- Read or tell stories with memorable characters before this activity to stimulate children's creativity.

DEVELOPMENTAL GOALS

Develop creativity and small muscles in hands and fingers; use familiar objects in new ways; and learn the design concepts of detail placement, color, and line.

PREPARATION

Wash the foam trays. Give each child one tray.

PROCESS

1. Choose a favorite story character, or imagine one.
2. Draw the character on the foam tray with markers.
3. Add yarn for hair, buttons for eyes, and so on.
4. Glue a stick to the bottom of the tray to work the puppet.

VARIATIONS

- Spread areas of the tray with glue and sprinkle on glitter for added fun.
- Have older children work in groups to write their own stories, then create foam tray puppets to act those stories out.

NOTES FOR NEXT TIME: ______________________________

____

____

____

Folded-Paper Puppets

MATERIALS

- ☐ rectangles of construction paper
- ☐ crayons
- ☐ markers
- ☐ wiggly eyes (optional)

HELPFUL HINTS

- Have the children fold with you as you demonstrate.
- Children may need help folding the paper for this activity. Resist the temptation to fold the paper for the children. The children may need some help at the beginning, but let them do it themselves.

DEVELOPMENTAL GOALS

Develop creativity, small muscles in hands and fingers, and hand-eye coordination and use familiar objects in new ways.

PREPARATION

Give each child a rectangular piece of construction paper.

PROCESS

1. Fold the long rectangle into fourths, making a W.
2. The W is the puppet's body.
3. Draw eyes on the front of the W.
4. Or glue on wiggly eyes.
5. Cut a tongue from paper and glue the end of it in the puppet's mouth.
6. To use the puppet, put the thumb in the lower fold and put other fingers in the upper fold.

VARIATIONS

- Use green paper to make a frog with a big, red tongue.
- Use brown paper and make a forked tongue for a snake puppet.
- Glue on sequins and glitter for a sparkly snake or frog.

NOTES FOR NEXT TIME: ______________________________

____

____

____

Food Puppets

MATERIALS

- ☐ apples, potatoes, or any other fruit or vegetable
- ☐ clothespins
- ☐ buttons
- ☐ old jewelry pieces
- ☐ yarn
- ☐ glue
- ☐ toothpicks
- ☐ scraps of fabric and trim

HELPFUL HINTS

- Attach details with small pieces of toothpicks.
- Food puppets have limited shelf lives. Be sure to dispose of the puppets before they get moldy.

DEVELOPMENTAL GOALS

Develop creativity, see familiar things in new ways, gain small motor practice of hands and fingers, and encourage imagination.

PREPARATION

Give each child one piece of fruit or vegetable.

PROCESS

1. Use the piece of fruit or vegetable for the puppet's head.
2. Insert a clothespin into the piece of fruit or vegetable for a handle.
3. Glue buttons, pins, or old jewelry pieces to the fruit or vegetable to make a face.
4. Glue yarn to the fruit or vegetable for hair.

VARIATIONS

- Use bits of cloth or an old sock as a dress or suit.
- Use whole cloves as nice-smelling details on an apple-head puppet.
- Use raisins and seeds for details.

NOTES FOR NEXT TIME: ________________________________

____

____

____

Glove Puppets

MATERIALS

- ☐ gloves
- ☐ large pom-poms
- ☐ scraps of felt
- ☐ glue
- ☐ scissors

- Glove puppets are a great way to recycle stray gloves.
- Heavy cotton garden gloves are inexpensive and work very well for this activity.

DEVELOPMENTAL GOALS

Develop creativity, small muscles in hands and fingers, and hand-eye coordination and use familiar objects in new ways.

PREPARATION

Give each child a glove. Discuss how each finger can be made into a finger puppet. Let the child try on the glove and move the fingers like five little puppets.

PROCESS

1. Glue pom-poms to each finger of the glove for the head.
2. Glue bits of felt or other fabric to the glove for facial or character details.
3. Let the glue dry, then enjoy!

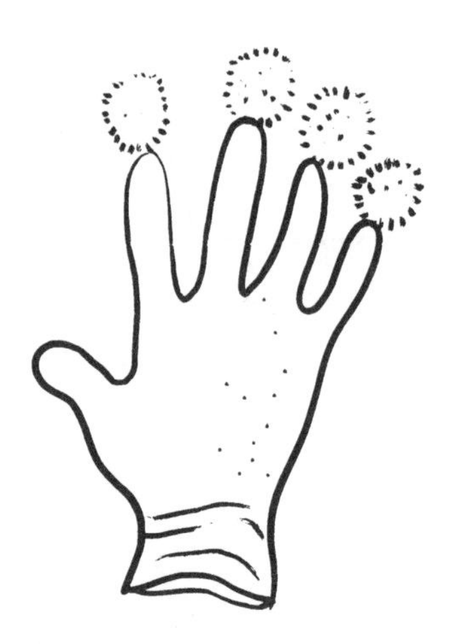

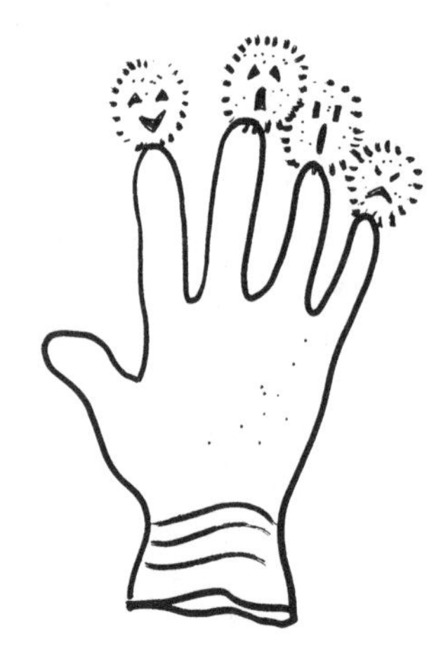

VARIATIONS

- Use old rubber gloves. Draw features on the rubber with felt-tip pens.
- Use garden gloves, and draw faces on the fabric.

NOTES FOR NEXT TIME: ______________________________

____

____

____

Handkerchief Puppets

MATERIALS

- ☐ handkerchiefs
- ☐ markers
- ☐ cotton balls
- ☐ rubber band or string

HELPFUL HINTS

- Because handkerchief puppets are so simple to make and use, they are excellent for very young children.
- Be prepared for children who finish their puppets quickly. Have enough materials for the children to make others.

DEVELOPMENTAL GOALS

Develop creativity and small muscles in fingers and hands, use familiar objects in new ways, and encourage dramatic play.

PREPARATION

Give each child a handkerchief.

PROCESS

1. Draw a face in the center of the handkerchief.
2. Stuff cotton or cloth inside the handkerchief, making the head.
3. Fasten the head with a piece of string or a rubber band.
4. Put the index finger in the head to work the puppet.

VARIATIONS

- Make a handkerchief puppet for each finger.
- Squares of muslin work as well as handkerchiefs.

NOTES FOR NEXT TIME: ___________________________

Humanettes

MATERIALS

- ☐ grocery bags
- ☐ crayons
- ☐ markers
- ☐ paint
- ☐ paintbrushes
- ☐ scraps of material, trim, yarn
- ☐ glue

HELPFUL HINTS

- Turn the bag upward slightly above the shoulder or cut arm holes in the bag's sides.
- People puppets help children transition from puppetry to creative drama.
- A shy child may feel most protected behind a humanette.
- For children who do not like their heads covered, do not force them to use humanettes.

DEVELOPMENTAL GOALS

Develop creativity and small muscles in fingers and hands; encourage dramatic play; and learn the design concepts of color, detail placement, and line.

PREPARATION

Explain that humanettes are half-people and half-puppets.

PROCESS

1. Give each child a large grocery bag.
2. Identify locations for eye and mouth holes.
3. Cut eye and mouth holes.
4. Add facial features with markers, crayons, or paint.
5. Decorate with cut-out pieces of paper and scraps of fabric and yarn.
6. Place the bag over the head to become a puppet.

VARIATIONS

- Make imaginary animals using the grocery bags.
- Act out a story or a fingerplay wearing a humanette.

NOTES FOR NEXT TIME: ______________________________

____

____

____

Juice-Box Puppets

MATERIALS

- ☐ juice boxes
- ☐ pipe cleaners
- ☐ scraps of felt
- ☐ tacky craft glue
- ☐ buttons
- ☐ Styrofoam ball (approximately 3 inches wide)
- ☐ yarn
- ☐ white pom-poms or small cotton balls
- ☐ scissors
- ☐ 3/8-inch dowel rod (8-inches long)

HELPFUL HINT

- When wooden dowels are unavailable, pencils work just as well.

NOTES FOR NEXT TIME:

____

____

____

____

DEVELOPMENTAL GOALS

Develop creativity and small muscles in fingers and hands; use familiar objects in new ways; appreciate recycling; and learn the design concepts of detail placement, color, symmetry, and patterning.

PREPARATION

Wash and dry empty juice cartons. For each puppet, cut a dowel so that it extends about 3 1/2 inches at the bottom of the juice box and about 1 inch at the top.

PROCESS

1. Cut slits at the top and bottom of the juice box to put the dowel through.
2. Be sure the dowel extends about 3 1/2 inches at the bottom for a handle and 1 inch at the top for the head.
3. Press the Styrofoam ball onto the dowel for the puppet's head.
4. Cut small slits on sides of box and insert a pipe cleaner through.
5. Twist the ends to create a circle for hands.
6. Glue on bits of felt for facial details.
7. Glue on wiggly eyes or bits of felt for eyes.
8. Color on hair with markers or glue on yarn for hair.
9. Glue on scraps of fabric for clothes.

VARIATIONS

- Make juice-box animals.
- Have a puppet show with the juice-box puppets.
- Make juice-box puppets of favorite book characters. Then, act out the book.

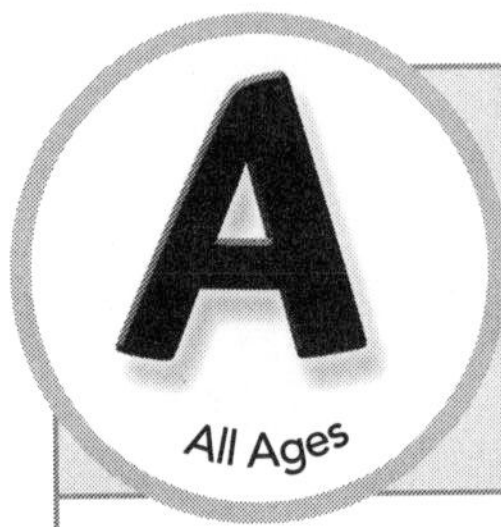

Me Puppets

MATERIALS

- ☐ current pictures of children's faces
- ☐ poster board
- ☐ markers
- ☐ scissors
- ☐ glue
- ☐ glitter

HELPFUL HINTS

- Do this activity at the beginning of the year and at the end of the year. Note the differences in the photos.
- Choose one or two children's me-puppets to focus on per week (or per day) as a way to get to know the children better. Let the puppets talk about themselves at group time or whenever appropriate in the day.

DEVELOPMENTAL GOALS

Develop creativity, small muscles in hands and fingers, and hand-eye coordination and encourage self-awareness and awareness of others.

PREPARATION

Collect current pictures of children's faces.

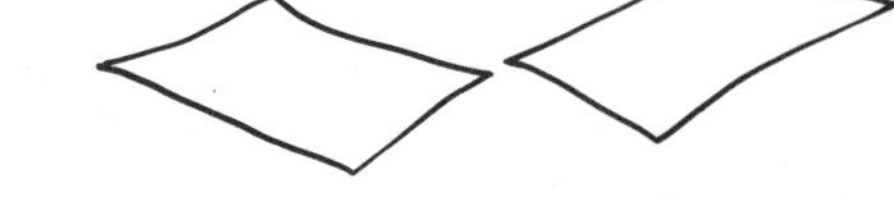

PROCESS

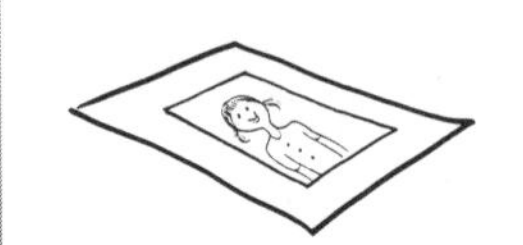

1. Measure two matching rectangles of poster board that are slightly larger than the child's picture.
2. Mark and cut out the rectangles with scissors.
3. On one rectangle, attach the child's picture with glue.
4. On the other rectangle, write the child's name with marker.
5. Make the name really fanciful with colored markers.
6. Make the area around the picture fancy, too.
7. Let the rectangle dry overnight.
8. Glue a wide craft stick between the two rectangles with the picture and name facing out.
9. Let the rectangle dry overnight.

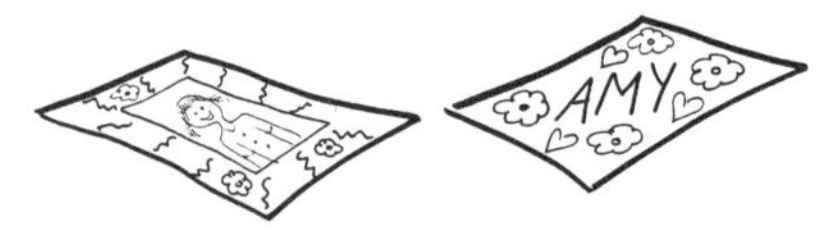

VARIATIONS

- Use pictures of the children when they were younger. See if the children can identify the children in the pictures.
- Spread glue and sprinkle glitter around the picture for a sparkly frame.
- If parents cannot provide pictures, buy a throw-away camera and take the children's pictures.

NOTES FOR NEXT TIME: ______________________________

____

____

____

Milk-Carton Puppets

MATERIALS

- ☐ one pint milk or cream carton
- ☐ construction paper
- ☐ markers
- ☐ glue
- ☐ scissors
- ☐ crayons

HELPFUL HINTS

- Older children may want to choose animals to make using the cartons. They can use a science book as a reference for details on their carton puppets.
- Older children may enjoy making imaginary creatures, then keeping journals of the creatures' adventures on earth and on other planets.

DEVELOPMENTAL GOALS

Develop creativity and small muscles in hands and fingers; use familiar objects in new ways; and learn the design concepts of detail placement, symmetry, and color.

PREPARATION

Wash the milk carton with hot, soapy water. Rinse and let dry. Cut a hole in the bottom of the carton large enough to put four fingers in to work the puppet. Talk about the kind of puppet the children can make from the milk carton. Discuss animals, people, objects, and imaginary things.

PROCESS

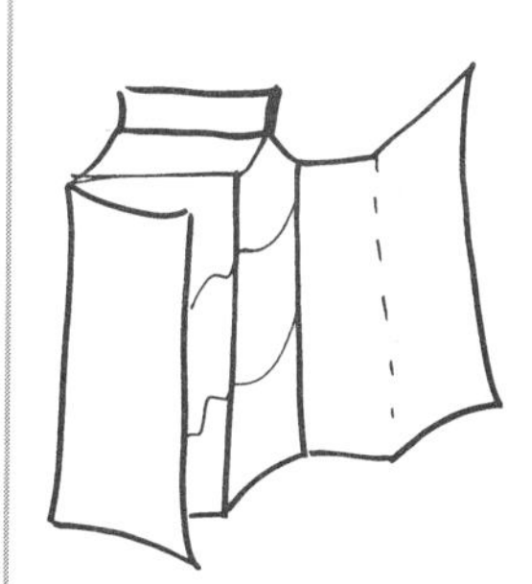

1. Cover the top and sides of the carton with construction paper.
2. For people or animals, glue feet near the bottom of the carton.
3. Cut out ears and glue them to the top of the carton.
4. Use markers or crayons on all sides of the carton to draw the animal's or person's hair.
5. For an animal, glue on a tail at the end of the carton.

VARIATIONS

- Make an imaginary visitor from the moon or another planet. Have the visitor tell its name. Tell about where it lives and what it is like to live there.
- For animals, use buttons for eyes, a scrap of felt for a tail, and a large pom-pom for a nose.
- Cover the carton with brown paper from a grocery bag. Draw on details with markers and crayons.

NOTES FOR NEXT TIME: ______________________________

____

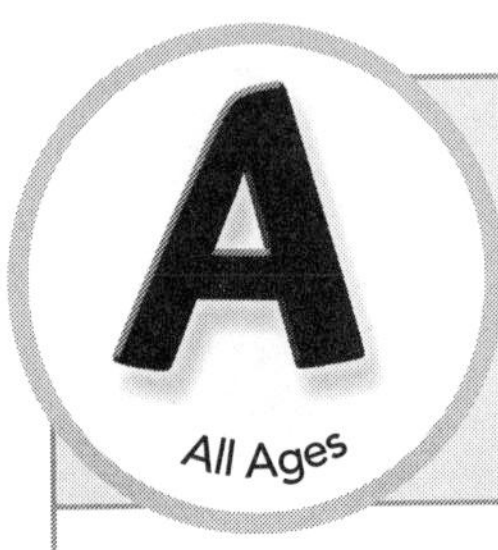

Mitten Puppets

MATERIALS

- ☐ old mittens
- ☐ glue
- ☐ buttons
- ☐ scrap pieces of felt, fabric, ribbon, trim, and yarn

- Mitten puppets are very easy to make and use. They are great for the youngest puppeteers.
- Mitten puppets make great use of single, worn-out, and outgrown mittens.

DEVELOPMENTAL GOALS

Develop creativity, small muscles in hands and fingers, and hand-eye coordination; use familiar objects in new ways; and encourage dramatic play.

PREPARATION

Collect lost-and-found mittens or mittens the children have outgrown.

PROCESS

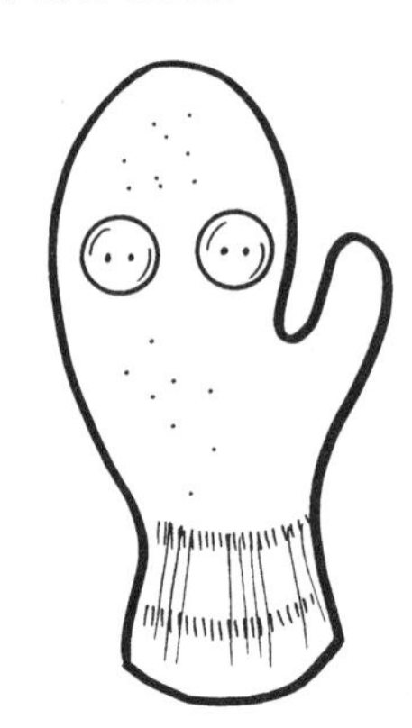

1. Give each child a mitten.
2. Glue buttons to the mitten for eyes.
3. Glue a scrap piece of felt or another button to the mitten as a nose.
4. Glue another piece of felt to the mitten as the mouth.
5. Slip the hand into the mitten and make the puppet talk by moving the thumb upward and downward against the four fingers.

VARIATIONS

- Glue yarn to the mitten as hair.
- Dress the mitten puppet with scraps of fabric for a hat, a dress, a coat, and so on.
- Make a mitten puppet for each hand. Have a puppet conversation.

NOTES FOR NEXT TIME: ______________________________

____

____

____

Nursery-Rhyme Finger Puppets

MATERIALS

- ☐ stiff paper, like construction paper or even thicker if available
- ☐ scissors
- ☐ markers
- ☐ crayons
- ☐ wiggly eyes (optional)
- ☐ glue
- ☐ cotton balls
- ☐ bits of yarn

HELPFUL HINT

- This activity is most appropriate for children who can use scissors.

DEVELOPMENTAL GOALS

Develop creativity, small muscles in hands and fingers, and hand-eye coordination and practice language skills.

PREPARATION

Review nursery rhymes, such as Jack and Jill, Humpty Dumpty, and Peter, Peter, Pumpkin Eater.

PROCESS

1. Using stiff paper, draw out a puppet for a nursery rhyme.
2. Draw the puppet large enough so two fingers can be placed into the bottom of the figure.
3. Cut out the finger puppet and the finger hole(s).
4. Glue on wiggly eyes or draw on eyes.
5. Add cotton-ball or yarn hair.
6. Put fingers through the puppet to use it.

VARIATIONS

- Make finger puppets of storybook or comic book characters.
- Act out nursery rhymes with the finger puppets.
- Have the finger puppets talk about what it is like to be the characters.
- Let the children ask the puppet questions.
- Have older children make up nursery-rhyme puppets for younger children's use, or have the older children put on a puppet play for the younger children.

NOTES FOR NEXT TIME: ______________________________________

____

____

Paper-Bag Zoo Creatures

MATERIALS

- ☐ small paper lunch bags
- ☐ scraps of construction paper
- ☐ glue
- ☐ scissors
- ☐ markers
- ☐ crayons
- ☐ wiggly eyes (optional)
- ☐ pipe cleaners (optional)

HELPFUL HINTS

- This is a good activity for before or after a field trip to the zoo.
- Do not overlook imaginary animals. They count, too!

DEVELOPMENTAL GOALS

Develop creativity, small muscles in fingers and hands, and hand-eye coordination; use familiar objects in new ways; and learn the design concept of detail placement.

PREPARATION

Give each child a small paper lunch bag.

PROCESS

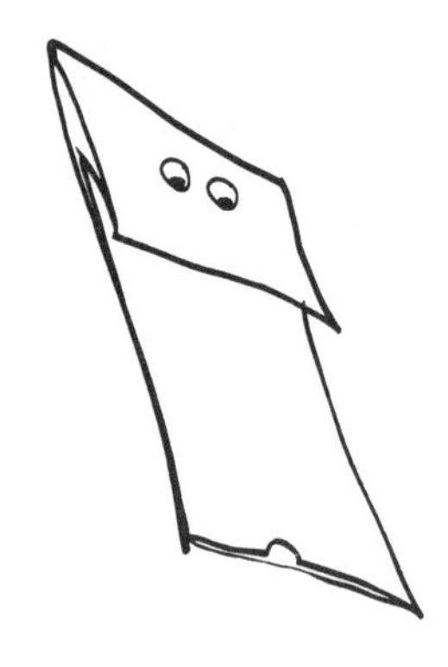

1. Cut out eyes from scraps of construction paper or use wiggly eyes.
2. Glue the eyes to the middle of the square on the bottom of the bag.
3. Glue a long tongue cut out of paper to the bottom of the square part of the bag.
4. Glue arms and legs to the sides of the bag.
5. Decorate the bag's front and back with crayons, markers, or glued-on pieces of construction paper.

VARIATIONS

- Fold the two square edges of a paper bag under to form a different shaped head.
- Cut out different shaped ears to make different animals: long, pink ears for a rabbit; round, black ears for a panda; brown, floppy ears for a dog; round gray ears for a mouse.
- Thread pipe cleaners through the paper bag for whiskers for cats and mice.
- Use white lunch bags to make a panda, a polar bear, a pig, and a bunny.

NOTES FOR NEXT TIME: ____________________

Paper-Chain Puppets

MATERIALS

- ☐ construction paper
- ☐ scissors
- ☐ glue
- ☐ markers or crayons
- ☐ string

HELPFUL HINTS

- For young children with short attention spans, use fewer strips for shorter chains.
- Be sure to stand back and let the children glue their own strips together. They may take longer than you, but it is important that they do it themselves.

NOTES FOR NEXT TIME:

____

____

____

DEVELOPMENTAL GOALS

Develop creativity, hand-eye coordination, and small muscles in fingers and hands and learn the design concepts of line, circles, color, and detail placement.

PREPARATION

Talk about insects and animals that are long and circular. Discuss such details as color, eyes, and if they have scales. Then, cut out 13 strips of paper that are 1 inch by 6 inches and one strip that is 4 inches square.

PROCESS

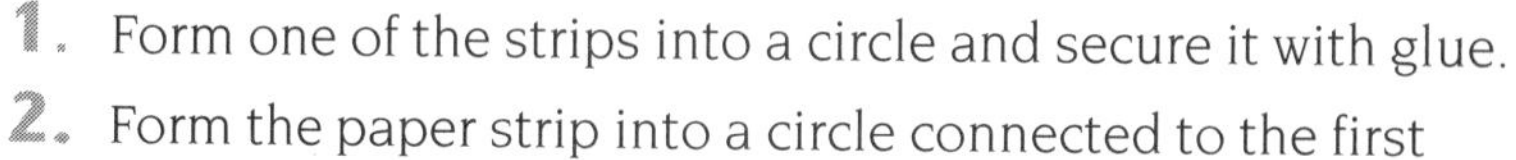

1. Form one of the strips into a circle and secure it with glue.
2. Form the paper strip into a circle connected to the first loop.
3. Continue until all 13 circles are connected, making a chain.
4. Each loop is a segment of the caterpillar.
5. Cut a circle from the paper square to make a head for the caterpillar.
6. Use markers or crayons to add eyes to the head.
7. Glue the head to one end of the chain.
8. Tie one piece of string to the head and another to the other end.
9. Use the string to move the chain as a puppet.

VARIATIONS

- Make paper-chain snakes, caterpillars, and even make-believe, snake-like creatures.
- Create an imaginary chain-thing from another planet. Name it. Let it tell the children all about itself.
- Make a nice, big paper-chain caterpillar. Make a nice, big leaf for the caterpillar to eat and rest on.
- Decorate each of the paper strips with crayons and markers for a very special puppet!
- Spread on glue and sprinkle on glitter for a sparkly chain puppet.

Paper-Plate Bugs and Stuff

MATERIALS

- ☐ paper plates
- ☐ scissors
- ☐ tape
- ☐ paint
- ☐ markers or crayons
- ☐ pipe cleaners
- ☐ hole punch
- ☐ buttons
- ☐ sequins

HELPFUL HINTS

- This activity is appropriate for children ages 5 and up.
- Encourage the children to create bugs that are unique.

NOTES FOR NEXT TIME:

____

____

____

____

DEVELOPMENTAL GOALS

Develop creativity, small muscles in fingers and hands, and hand-eye coordination; use familiar objects in new ways; and learn the design concepts of detail placement, color, pattern, and symmetry.

PREPARATION

Talk about bugs. Discuss their sizes, shapes, colors, and such details as eyes, antennae, legs, and wings. Give each child two paper plates.

PROCESS

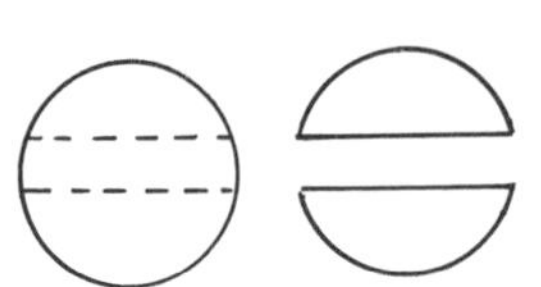

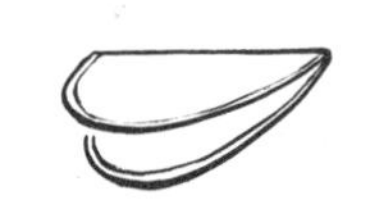

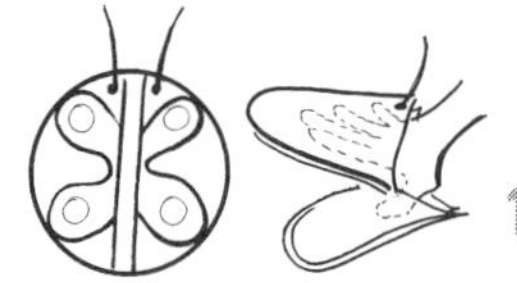

1. Fold a paper plate in half (fold it so that the back side of the plate is touching itself).
2. Using another paper plate, cut out a strip of the plate from the middle. Discard the middle strip.

3. Tape or staple each of the half-round pieces you just cut to the folded plate.
4. Position the plates so that the eating surfaces of the plates are facing each other.

5. Tape along the round edges only.

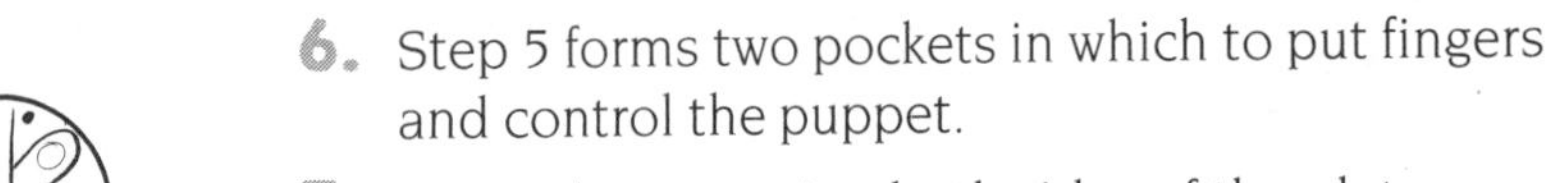

6. Step 5 forms two pockets in which to put fingers and control the puppet.

7. Draw a bug covering both sides of the plate.

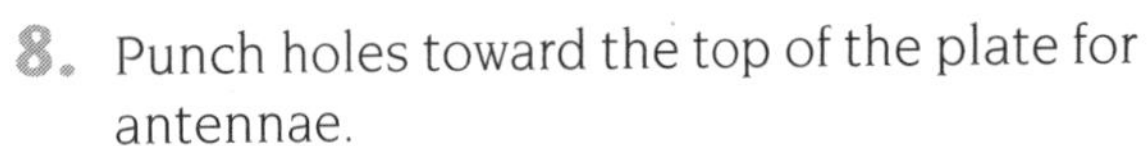

8. Punch holes toward the top of the plate for antennae.
9. Loop a pipe cleaner through the holes for the antennae.
10. Slip the thumb and fingers into the pockets and bring the bug to life!

VARIATIONS

- Create an insect that has never been seen before. Name it. Have it tell everyone where it is from and what its life is like there.
- Make a paper-plate butterfly.
- Spread glue on part of the bug design and sprinkle glitter on the glue.
- Glue on buttons for eyes and sequins for shiny scales.

Paper-Plate Puppets

MATERIALS

- ☐ paper plates
- ☐ Popsicle sticks
- ☐ stapler and staples
- ☐ crayons
- ☐ markers
- ☐ fabric scraps
- ☐ trim
- ☐ wallpaper
- ☐ yarn
- ☐ buttons
- ☐ paste
- ☐ construction paper

HELPFUL HINTS

- Move the plate along a table edge as a puppet, or use it as a mask.
- Do not use sequins and beads for children under 3 years old.

DEVELOPMENTAL GOALS

Develop creative thinking, small motor skills in the hands and fingers, and hand-eye coordination; understand the concepts of color, contrast, and detail; and encourage imagination.

PREPARATION

Give each child a paper plate.

PROCESS

1. Make a face on the paper plate with crayons, paint, or glued-on colored-paper pieces.
2. Staple a Popsicle stick to the bottom of the plate for a handle.
3. Add such details as yarn for hair, buttons for eyes, and sequins for earrings.

VARIATIONS

- Make a hole for a mouth so the child can use one finger as a tongue to make the puppet talk.
- Make paper-plate animals for an imaginary zoo story.
- Have older children make paper-plate puppets of favorite storybook or fairy-tale characters.

NOTES FOR NEXT TIME: ______________________________

Paper-Tube Puppets

MATERIALS

- ☐ paper tubes from paper towels or toilet tissue
- ☐ paste
- ☐ scraps of fabric, yarn, ribbon, and trim
- ☐ small Styrofoam balls
- ☐ buttons
- ☐ pom-poms
- ☐ feathers
- ☐ glue

HELPFUL HINTS

- Slip the puppet over one or two fingers to make it come alive.
- Cut paper tubes in varying lengths so the puppets can be all sizes.

DEVELOPMENTAL GOALS

Develop creativity and small muscles in hands and fingers; use familiar objects in new ways; and learn the design concepts of detail placement, color, and variety.

PREPARATION

Give each child a paper tube. Talk about what kinds of puppets the children could make. Discuss such features as eyes, noses, mouths, and hair.

PROCESS

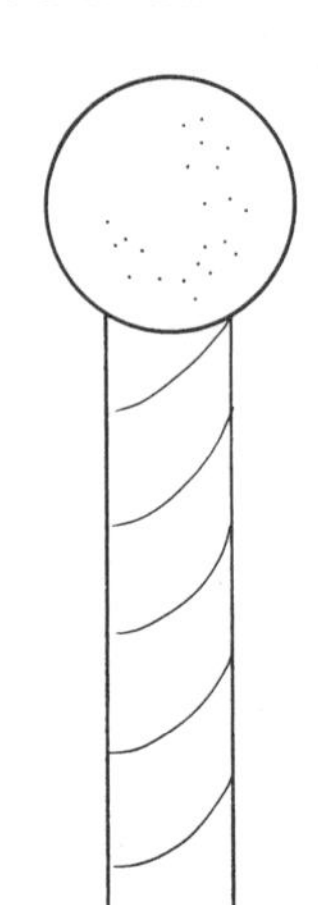

1. The paper tube is the body.
2. Glue the Styrofoam ball to the tube to become the head.
3. Glue buttons to the ball for eyes.
4. Glue pom-poms to the ball for a nose or ears.
5. Decorate with pieces of trim for hair, hats, or other details.

VARIATIONS

- Make paper-tube animals. Sing "Farmer in the Dell" with the tube animals as the chorus.
- Make a family of tube puppets. Use the puppets to act out family stories.
- Have older children make their favorite fairy-tale or storybook characters.

NOTES FOR NEXT TIME: ______________________________

____

____

____

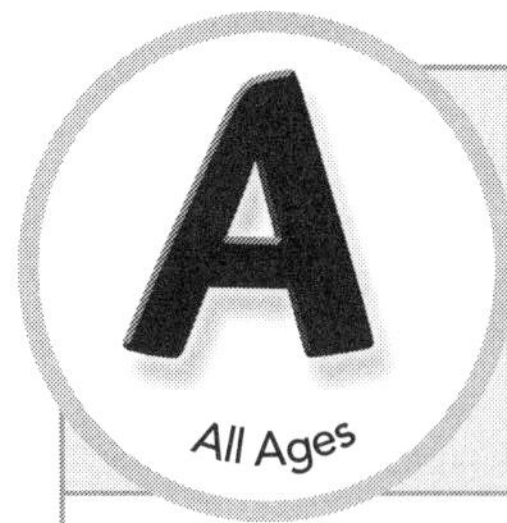

Paper/Styrofoam Cup Puppets

MATERIALS

- ☐ paper/ Styrofoam cups
- ☐ markers
- ☐ pipe cleaners
- ☐ scraps of yarn, fabric, and trim
- ☐ construction paper
- ☐ glue

HELPFUL HINTS

- Paper/Styrofoam cup puppets are great for all children, even toddlers, because they are very easy to make and use.
- Markers work best on Styrofoam. Crayons do not work well on Styrofoam.

DEVELOPMENTAL GOALS

Develop creativity, hand-eye coordination, and small muscles in fingers and hands; use familiar objects in new ways; and encourage imagination.

PREPARATION

Give each child a paper or Styrofoam cup.

PROCESS

1. Draw a face on the cup.
2. Or glue paper eyes, a nose, and a mouth on the cup.
3. Add yarn for hair.

VARIATIONS

- Make an animal by gluing ears to the top of the cup and a pipe-cleaner or paper-strip tail to the back.
- Create a family of cup puppets.
- Have older children create their favorite cartoon or storybook characters.

NOTES FOR NEXT TIME: ______________________________

____

____

____

Pencil Puppets

MATERIALS

- ☐ pencils
- ☐ construction paper
- ☐ paste
- ☐ scraps of felt, fabric, and trim
- ☐ scissors

- Cut figures from comics or magazines instead of drawing figures.

DEVELOPMENTAL GOALS

Develop creativity, small muscles in fingers and hands, hand-eye coordination and use familiar objects in new ways.

PREPARATION

Discuss the children's favorite characters and animals. Choose one favorite.

PROCESS

1. Draw the character on construction paper.
2. Cut the character out.
3. Glue on pieces of felt for facial details.
4. Glue on pieces of fabric for clothing.
5. Glue the character to a pencil.
6. Let the glue dry thoroughly before using the puppet.

VARIATIONS

- Make three little pigs as pencil puppets. Act out the story using these puppets.
- Make three bears as pencil puppets. Act out this story using the puppets.
- Older children may enjoy making pencil puppets for favorite stories. Have the children act out the story.

NOTES FOR NEXT TIME: ______________________________

____

____

____

Ping-Pong Ball Puppets

MATERIALS

- ☐ ping-pong balls
- ☐ fabric scraps
- ☐ glue
- ☐ markers
- ☐ paste
- ☐ construction paper

HELPFUL HINTS

- Use the ping-pong ball puppet as a finger puppet.
- Make sure the X shape is large enough to be comfortable but not too large as to make the puppet fall off.

DEVELOPMENTAL GOALS

Develop creativity, small muscles in hands and fingers, and hand-eye coordination; use familiar objects in new ways; and encourage imagination.

PREPARATION

Cut an "X" out of a ping-pong ball using sharp scissors.

PROCESS

1. Place a piece of lightweight fabric on a finger.
2. Cover the X area of the ball with sturdy glue.
3. Force the ball onto the fabric on your finger at the X.
4. Take the ball and fabric off your finger and let the glue dry.
5. While the glue is drying, draw or paste cut-out pieces of construction paper onto the puppet.

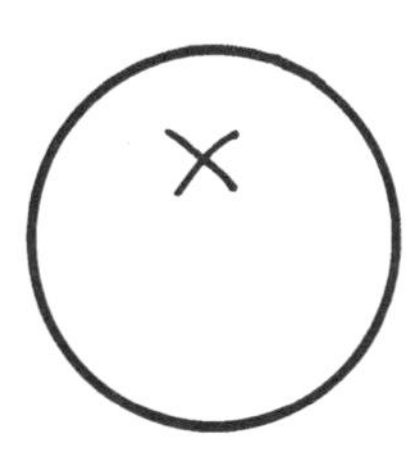

VARIATIONS

- Use old tennis balls instead of ping-pong balls.
- Have a pretend ping-pong game with these puppets. Have a ping-pong audience cheer the players on!

NOTES FOR NEXT TIME: ______________________________

____

____

____

Play Dough Puppets

MATERIALS

- ☐ play dough
- ☐ round cereal pieces
- ☐ raisins

- Be careful with very young children, because they may try to put inappropriate things in their mouths.
- Expect the young artists to "nibble" on the decorative elements before using them on the puppet. This is part of the fun!

DEVELOPMENTAL GOALS

Develop creativity, small muscles in fingers and hands, and hand-eye coordination; use play dough in new ways; and encourage imagination.

PREPARATION

Give each child a small amount of play dough.

PROCESS

1. Place a small amount of play dough on a finger.
2. Mold the play dough into a face shape covering the finger.
3. Add raisins, cereal, and so on for facial features.
4. The puppet is ready for play.

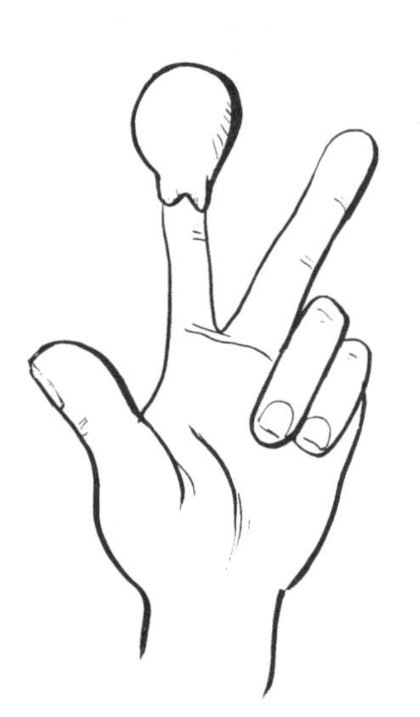

VARIATIONS

- Make a play dough puppet for each finger.
- Let the children make play dough puppets on each others' fingers.

NOTES FOR NEXT TIME: ______________________________

Pom-Pom Puppets

MATERIALS

- ☐ pom-poms of varying sizes and colors
- ☐ Popsicle or craft sticks
- ☐ paste
- ☐ hole punch
- ☐ construction paper
- ☐ scraps of fabric, yarn, and trim

HELPFUL HINTS

- This activity requires some degree of small motor control, because the pom-poms are small and difficult to handle.
- Have a good supply of pom-poms and sticks available for children who finish the puppet quickly. Fast children can make several.

DEVELOPMENTAL GOALS

Develop creativity, small muscles in hands and fingers, and hand-eye coordination and learn the design concepts of pattern, symmetry, and details.

PREPARATION

Talk about the pom-poms. Discuss what kind of puppets could be made with them. Talk about colors, details, features, and so on.

PROCESS

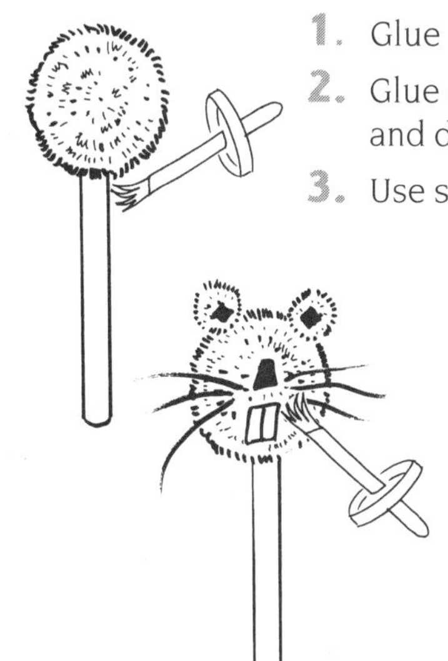

1. Glue a large pom-pom to the stick.
2. Glue on pieces of construction paper for features and details.
3. Use smaller pom-poms for other details.
4. Use a hole punch on colored construction paper.
5. Glue on the colored circles from the hole punch, if desired.
6. Add fabric strips to the stick for clothing.
7. Glue on yarn for hair.

VARIATIONS

- Make a group of pom-pom puppets for a group singalong. Let the children choose the songs.
- Make animals for the song "Farmer in the Dell" and use them as you sing the song.
- Use cotton balls instead of pom-poms, but be aware that cotton balls are less stable decorations.

NOTES FOR NEXT TIME: ______________________________

____

____

3

Years Old and Up

Popsicle-Stick Puppets

MATERIALS

- ☐ Popsicle sticks
- ☐ scraps of fabric, yarn, and trim
- ☐ scissors
- ☐ white glue
- ☐ fine-point colored markers
- ☐ wiggle eyes (optional)

HELPFUL HINT

- You may have to show the children how to glue the fabric in place on the stick, but do not glue for them. Guide the children as they glue.

NOTES FOR NEXT TIME:

____

____

____

____

DEVELOPMENTAL GOALS

Develop creativity, small muscles in hands and fingers, and hand-eye coordination and use familiar objects in new ways.

PREPARATION

Talk about the kinds of puppets the children could make using Popsicle sticks. Discuss how the puppets could be mothers, fathers, kids, animals, and so on. Cut fabric into small scraps two to three times as wide as the Popsicle stick.

PROCESS

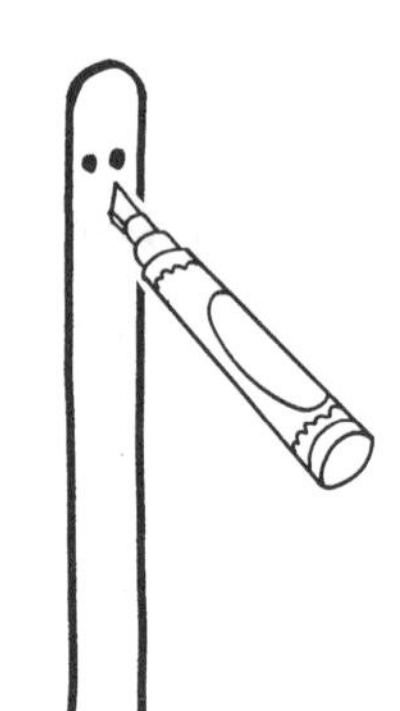

1. Give each child a Popsicle stick.
2. Draw eyes at the top of the stick or glue on wiggle eyes.
3. Be sure to leave enough room for hair or a hat.
4. Place a dot or two of glue on front of the stick, and place material on the glue.
5. Secure the material and wrap it around the stick, gluing it in place at the back of the stick.
6. Add such details as yarn hair to the top.
7. Glue a piece of ribbon as a belt in the middle of the stick.
8. Use markers to add facial details.

VARIATIONS

- Make a family of stick puppets. Act out a familiar family scene, such as mealtime or going to the store.
- Create the characters from a favorite story. Use the stick puppets to act out the story.
- Make a "mystery guest" stick puppet. Let the other children guess its identity.

Pop-Up Puppets

MATERIALS

- ☐ paper or Styrofoam puppets
- ☐ craft or Popsicle sticks
- ☐ construction paper
- ☐ paste
- ☐ crayons
- ☐ markers
- ☐ pipe cleaners

HELPFUL HINTS

- Some children may need help putting the stick into the cup. Let the children help each other do this.
- You can use pencils for this activity as well.

DEVELOPMENTAL GOALS

Develop creativity, small muscles in hands and fingers, and hand-eye coordination.

PREPARATION

Poke a large hole through the bottom of the cup so that a craft or Popsicle stick will fit through it.

PROCESS

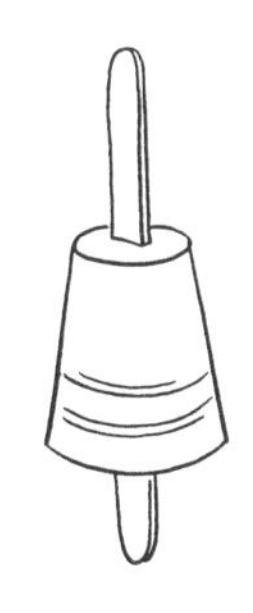

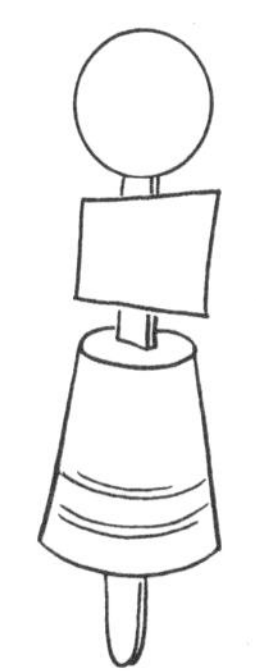

1. Give each child a cup and a craft or Popsicle stick.
2. Poke the stick through the hole in the cup and hold it so the top of the stick is a good deal above the top of the cup.
3. Tape a horizontal strip of construction paper to the stick for the puppet's body.
4. Use cut-out pieces of construction paper for the puppet's head.
5. Glue the head to the top of the stick.
6. Glue on pieces of pipe cleaners for arms.
7. Work the puppet by moving the stick up and down in the cup.

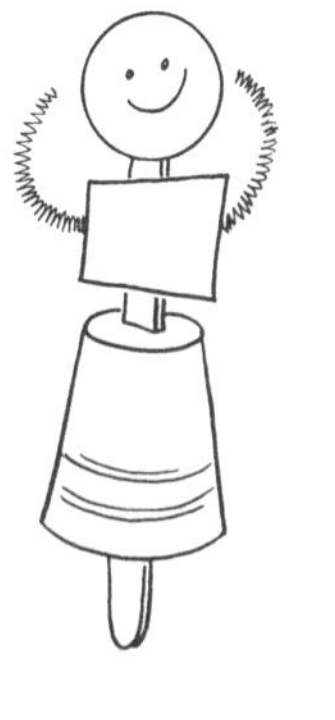

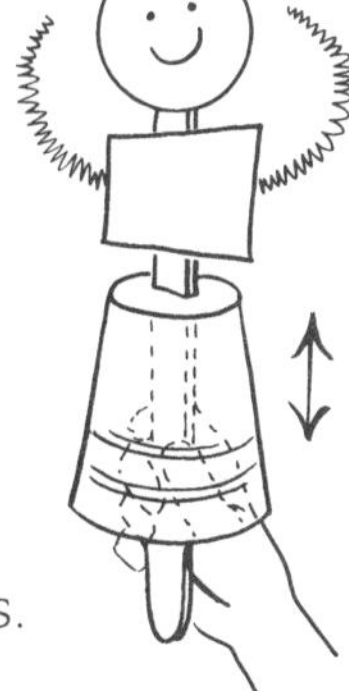

VARIATIONS

- Use cups of different sizes.
- Use fabric scraps for puppet's body.
- Make animal pop-up puppets.
- Act out fingerplays, rhymes, or poems with these puppets.

NOTES FOR NEXT TIME: ______________________________

____

____

____

Pringle™-Can Puppets

MATERIALS

- ☐ empty Pringle™ cans
- ☐ construction paper
- ☐ glue
- ☐ scissors
- ☐ scraps of fabric, yarn, trim
- ☐ beads (optional)
- ☐ feathers (optional)
- ☐ masking tape
- ☐ markers
- ☐ crayons
- ☐ paint
- ☐ paintbrushes

HELPFUL HINT

- Have friends save Pringle™ cans for this activity, or have the children bring them from home.

DEVELOPMENTAL GOALS

Develop creativity, small muscles in hands and fingers, and hand-eye coordination; use familiar objects in new ways; and learn the design concepts of detail placement, color, line, and symmetry.

PREPARATION

Talk about the kinds of puppets Pringle™ cans can make. Discuss how they could be people, animals, objects, and imaginary or storybook characters. Wash out and dry the Pringle™ cans. Cover the metal on the open end with masking tape where the hand goes in to work the puppet.

PROCESS

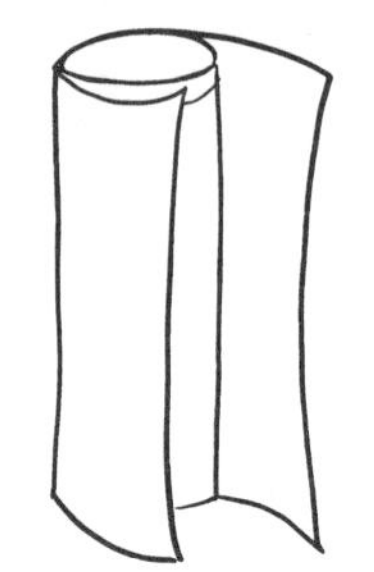

1. Give each child a Pringle™ can.
2. Glue construction paper on to cover the can.
3. Draw a face on the top (closed end) of the can.
4. Glue on yarn for hair.
5. Dress the puppet with fabric scraps and pieces of trim.
6. Glue on beads for eyes.

VARIATIONS

- Make favorite comic book, television, or storybook characters. Have the children act out a scene.
- Older children may want to make favorite historical characters. Have the other children guess who it is.
- Create a visitor from another planet. Have it tell you its name. Then, ask the creature questions about its home and how it is to live there.
- Make vegetable and fruit Pringle™ puppets. Put them together for a healthy meal. Have them talk about how they look, taste, and feel and why they are good for you.

NOTES FOR NEXT TIME: ______________________________

____

Shadow Puppets

MATERIALS

- ☐ heavy paper
- ☐ sticks
- ☐ glue or a stapler and staples
- ☐ a light source
- ☐ a blank wall area or screen

HELPFUL HINTS

- Even very young children can make and enjoy hand shadow puppets.
- The stronger the light, the clearer the shadows.
- A flashlight works well for a small wall area. For a larger area, you may need a lamp.

DEVELOPMENTAL GOALS

Develop creativity and small muscles in fingers and hands and encourage creative movement and dramatics.

PREPARATION

Talk about shadows. Observe shadows during an outdoor walk. Show the children how to make and see hand shadows on the wall.

PROCESS

1. Draw and cut out a figure from heavy paper. (Recycled white gift boxes work well.)
2. Attach a stick to the figure.
3. Shine a light on an area of open wall space.
4. Move the puppet to see its shadow on the wall.
5. Watch the puppet's size and shape change as the puppet's or light's position changes.

VARIATION

- Have some children use their hands for shadow puppets and stick puppets for shadow puppets. Compare how the puppets look. Let the puppets talk to each other as their shadows move on the wall.

NOTES FOR NEXT TIME: ______________________________

____

____

Shape Stick Puppets

MATERIALS

- ☐ construction paper
- ☐ cardboard or heavy-paper shapes
- ☐ scissors
- ☐ paste
- ☐ decorative items (e.g., beads, sequins, scraps of wallpaper, fabric, and trim)

HELPFUL HINT

- This activity is appropriate for children who can cut with scissors.

NOTES FOR NEXT TIME:

____

____

____

____

DEVELOPMENTAL GOALS

Develop creative thinking, shape recognition, and small motor skills; understand design line and shape concepts; and encourage imagination.

PREPARATION

Talk about shapes. Review the circle, triangle, square, and rectangle.

PROCESS

1. Trace shapes on construction paper.
2. Cut out the shapes.
3. Arrange the shapes into a figure.
4. Use a circle for the head.
5. Make the body from a triangle, square, or rectangle.

6. Cut arms and legs from construction paper.

7. When satisfied with the arrangement, glue it to construction paper.

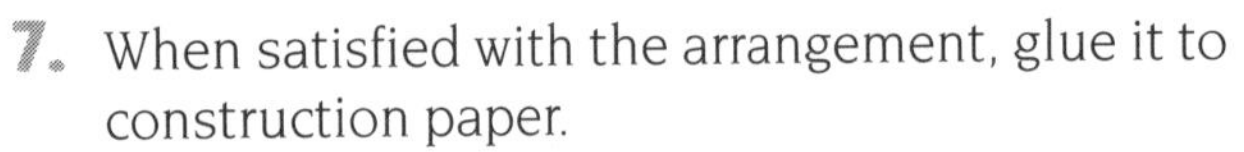

8. After the glue dries, cut the figure from the construction paper and decorate it with markers.

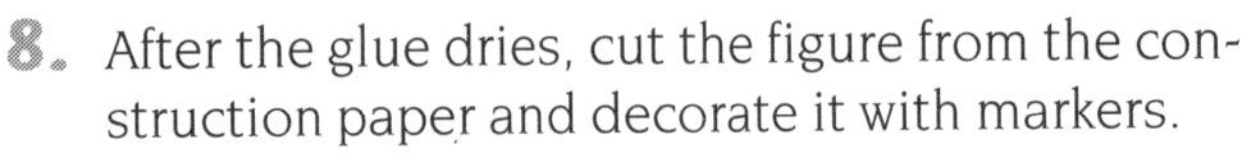

9. "Dress" the figure with scraps of fabric, wallpaper, and trim.
10. Glue the figure to a stick.

VARIATIONS

- Use pipe cleaners for arms and legs.
- Make shape animals.
- Make favorite cartoon or storybook characters.

Single-Bag Puppets

MATERIALS

- ☐ small paper lunch bags
- ☐ crayons
- ☐ markers
- ☐ paint
- ☐ paintbrushes
- ☐ glue
- ☐ yarn
- ☐ colored construction paper
- ☐ pieces of fabric, wallpaper, and trim

HELPFUL HINT

- This is a good first puppet for very young children. It is easy to make and easy to use.

DEVELOPMENTAL GOALS

Develop creativity and small motor skills, use familiar objects in new ways, and encourage imagination.

PREPARATION

Give each child a lunch bag.

PROCESS

1. On the bottom (square part) of the bag, draw facial features with crayons, markers, or paint to make the head.
2. Cut-out pieces of construction paper and glue them to the bag as other features.
3. Glue or staple on pieces of yarn for hair.
4. Decorate the rest of the bag as the puppet body.

VARIATIONS

- Make paper-bag animal puppets.
- Create a family of bag puppets.
- Make a paper-bag self-portrait.

NOTES FOR NEXT TIME: ______________________

Sock Puppets

MATERIALS

- ☐ old socks
- ☐ buttons
- ☐ scraps of felt, fabric, and trim
- ☐ glue

- Sock puppets are traditional but great to use and fun to make.
- Exaggerate the puppets' features. For example, make a long, red tongue for a snake. Give the sock puppet character.

DEVELOPMENTAL GOALS

Develop creativity and small muscles in fingers and hands, use familiar objects in new ways, and encourage dramatic play.

PREPARATION

Give each child an old sock.

PROCESS

1. Pull the sock over the hand.
2. Glue facial features to the toe of the sock.
3. Add other decorative touches, such as yarn for hair and trim for clothes.
4. Let the glue dry, then put the puppet on and play!

VARIATIONS

- Make sock snakes, dogs, cats, and other animals.
- Use socks with prints and argyle designs as well as solid-colored socks.

NOTES FOR NEXT TIME: ______________________________

Spool Puppets

MATERIALS

- ☐ spools
- ☐ pencils
- ☐ glue
- ☐ markers
- ☐ scraps of fabric, yarn, and trim

HELPFUL HINTS

- The only reason to sharpen the pencils is to fit them in the bottom of the spool.
- Be watchful of young children with pencils.

NOTES FOR NEXT TIME:

____

____

____

____

DEVELOPMENTAL GOALS

Develop creativity, small muscles in hands and fingers, and hand-eye coordination and use familiar objects in new ways.

PREPARATION

Talk about what kind of puppet a spool would make. Discuss people, animals, objects, and imaginary creatures. Sharpen pencils to a point.

PROCESS

1. Give each child a spool and a pencil.
2. Draw a face on the spool.
3. Draw ears on the sides of the spool.
4. Glue on bits of yarn for hair on top and sides of the spool.
5. Add fabric scraps for clothing.

6. Put glue in the bottom hole of the spool.
7. Insert the sharpened end of the pencil into the bottom hole of the spool.
8. Let the glue dry thoroughly, then use and enjoy!

VARIATIONS

- Use old ballpoint pens instead of pencils.
- Create spool characters to act out fingerplays.
- Create a spool city full of imaginary creatures that have exciting stories to tell.
- Use cone spools instead of regular thread spools for an interesting variation. See what type of cone-headed characters you can create!

Stuffed-Animal Stick Puppets

MATERIALS

- ☐ Popsicle sticks
- ☐ twigs
- ☐ pencils
- ☐ small stuffed animals
- ☐ yarn or rubber bands

HELPFUL HINTS

- Garage sales are good sources for stuffed animals.
- This is a good way to recycle old stuffed animals. Be sure to launder before using.

DEVELOPMENTAL GOALS

Develop creativity and small motor skills, see familiar things in new ways, and encourage imagination.

PREPARATION

Collect small stuffed animals.

PROCESS

1. Attach a small stuffed animal to a stick or a pencil with a piece of string or a rubber band.
2. Dress the puppet with scraps of fabric and trim.
3. Use this puppet like a stick puppet.

VARIATIONS

- Attach small dolls to sticks to make puppets.
- Act out a fairy tale or a favorite story with the stuffed-animal stick puppets.

NOTES FOR NEXT TIME: ______________________________

____

____

____

Styrofoam-Ball Puppets

MATERIALS

- ☐ Styrofoam balls
- ☐ felt-tip pens
- ☐ scraps of colored paper
- ☐ fabric, trim
- ☐ buttons
- ☐ glue
- ☐ pencil

HELPFUL HINT

- Felt-tip pens work best on Styrofoam. Crayons do not work well on Styrofoam.

DEVELOPMENTAL GOALS

Develop creativity, small muscles in fingers and hands, and hand-eye coordination; use familiar objects in new ways; and learn the design concepts of detail, color, and placement.

PREPARATION

Give each child a Styrofoam ball.

PROCESS

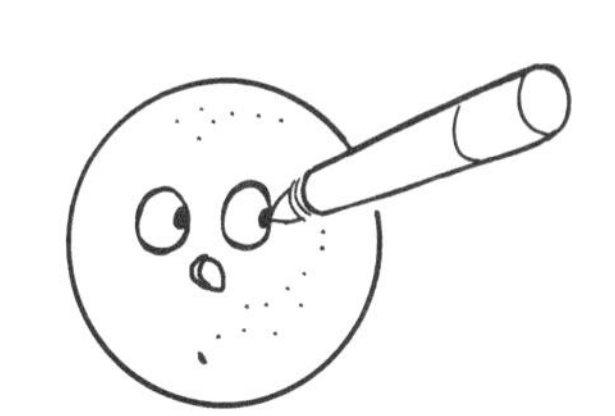

1. Make a face with felt-tip pens on the Styrofoam ball.
2. Or glue paper eyes, a nose, and a mouth to the ball.
3. Insert a pencil in the bottom of the ball for the puppet's handle.
4. Or make a hole in the Styrofoam ball in which to place a finger to work the puppet.

VARIATIONS

- Add such details as yarn for hair and buttons for eyes.
- Make real or imaginary animal Styrofoam-ball puppets.
- Create Styrofoam-ball puppets to use with fingerplays.

NOTES FOR NEXT TIME: ______________________________

____

____

____

Tissue Puppets

MATERIALS

- ☐ facial tissue
- ☐ sticks (e.g., Popsicle sticks, large twigs, pencils)
- ☐ cotton
- ☐ string, or rubber bands

HELPFUL HINTS

- Children may need some help securing the tissue to the stick.
- Make the string or the yarn used to fasten the head to the stick part of the tissue puppet's "costume" (e.g., a big bowtie made of yarn).
- Because tissue is a bit fragile, this material is most appropriate for children with the small motor development to handle this material.

DEVELOPMENTAL GOALS

Develop creativity, small motor skills, and hand-eye coordination and encourage imagination.

PREPARATION

Give each child two tissues (allow one for mistakes).

PROCESS

1. Place the tissue over the stick.
2. Stuff the tissue with cotton.
3. Attach the top of the tissue to the stick using string or a rubber band, making a head.
4. Draw a face on the head with markers.

VARIATIONS

- Make tissue "ghosts."
- Make a family of tissue puppets.
- Use the puppets to sing along with a favorite song.

NOTES FOR NEXT TIME: ______________________________

____

____

____

Two-Bag Puppets

MATERIALS

- ☐ paper bags
- ☐ crayons
- ☐ markers
- ☐ paint
- ☐ paintbrushes
- ☐ yarn
- ☐ buttons
- ☐ paste
- ☐ colored construction paper
- ☐ scraps of fabric, yarn, trim
- ☐ newspaper
- ☐ glue

HELPFUL HINT

- Encourage the children to search for the right materials for their puppets. The search is as much fun as the finished puppet!

DEVELOPMENTAL GOALS

Develop creativity, small motor skills in the fingers and hands, and hand-eye coordination and encourage imagination.

PREPARATION

Have the children crumple the newspaper into wads.

PROCESS

1. Give each child two paper bags: one for the head and one for the body.
2. Stuff one bag with wads of newspaper and staple or glue the bag shut. This is the head.
3. Make the body by stapling a second bag to the first. Leave room for the child's hand to slip in and work the puppet.
4. Make a face on the head with paint, crayons, or colored paper and paste.
5. "Dress" the body by gluing on scraps of fabric and trim.

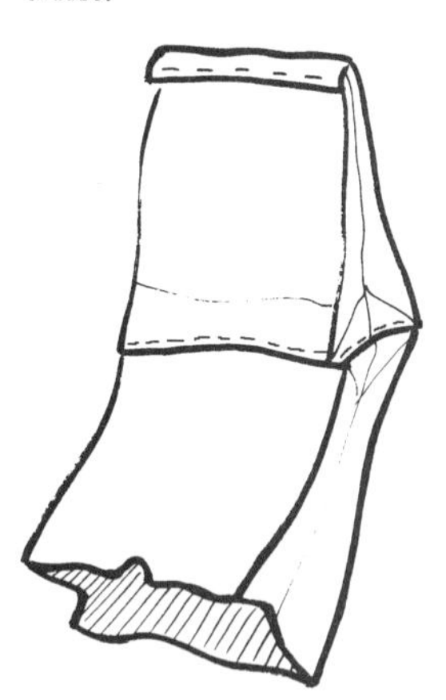

VARIATIONS

- Use buttons to make eyes, crumpled tissue to make a nose, and yarn to make hair.
- Make paper-bag animals, cartoon characters, and family members.

NOTES FOR NEXT TIME: ______________________________

Two-Faced Paper-Plate Puppets

MATERIALS

- ☐ white paper plates
- ☐ crayons
- ☐ markers
- ☐ Popsicle or craft sticks
- ☐ stapler and staples or glue
- ☐ buttons
- ☐ construction paper
- ☐ yarn

HELPFUL HINT

- Two-faced puppets are good to use when talking about feelings. For example, ask a child to use the puppet's face to show how it feels about having vegetable soup for lunch.

DEVELOPMENTAL GOALS

Develop creativity, small muscles in hands and fingers, and hand-eye coordination; use familiar objects in new ways; and learn the design concepts of color, detail placement, and line.

PREPARATION

Give each child two paper plates.

PROCESS

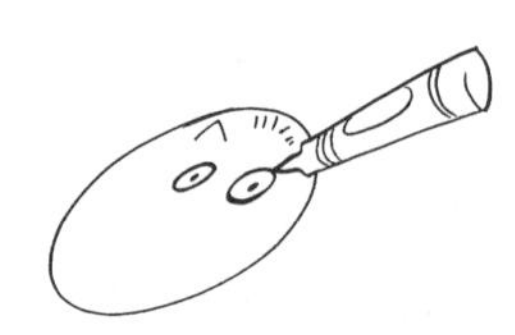

1. Draw a face on the back of each paper plate.
2. Add details to the plates with buttons, pieces of yarn, and pieces of construction paper.
3. Insert a stick between the paper plates and staple or glue it in place.
4. Staple the edges of the plates together.

VARIATIONS

- Make an animal face on the back of each plate.
- Make a happy face on one plate and a sad face on the other.

NOTES FOR NEXT TIME: ____________________

Uncanny Puppets

MATERIALS

- ☐ clean cans of various sizes with open rims taped
- ☐ paint
- ☐ brushes
- ☐ construction paper
- ☐ paste
- ☐ markers
- ☐ scraps of fabric, trim, and yarn
- ☐ scissors
- ☐ masking tape
- ☐ markers
- ☐ crayons

HELPFUL HINTS

- Small cans can be worked by putting two or three fingers inside. Larger cans can be worked by putting the whole hand inside.
- Some children may have trouble waiting for the glue to dry on the paper. You might let them paint directly onto the can and skip the pasting step.

DEVELOPMENTAL GOALS

Develop creativity, small muscles in fingers and hands, and hand-eye coordination; use familiar objects in new ways; and encourage recycling.

PREPARATION

Be sure to wash all cans and let them dry thoroughly. Tape the open ends of the can with masking tape to completely cover the ends. Discuss what kind of people, animals, objects, and imaginary creatures could be made from these cans. Talk about the sizes, shapes, and feel of the cans.

PROCESS

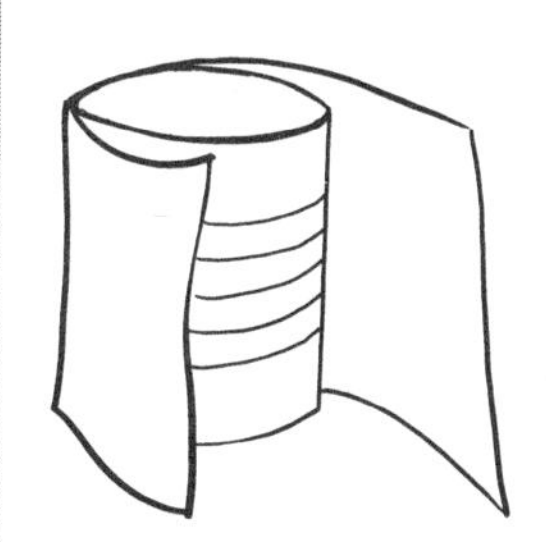

1. Give each child one can.
2. Spread glue on the can and cover it with construction paper.
3. Let the glue dry before decorating the can.
4. Draw on a face with crayons or markers.
5. Or make a face by gluing on pieces of construction paper.
6. Glue yarn hair to the top of the can.
7. Draw on clothing details or glue on fabric scraps for clothes.
8. Insert a hand into the bottom of the can to work the puppet.

VARIATIONS

- Use yogurt cups instead of tin cans for this activity.
- Make a family of can puppets with different sized cans. Act out a familiar family scene with these puppets.
- Make a "mystery" can puppet. Have the other children guess each other's puppets.
- Older children may enjoy making can puppets of favorite television, cartoon, or storybook characters.

NOTES FOR NEXT TIME: ______________________________

____

Wooden-Spoon Puppets

MATERIALS

- ☐ wooden spoons
- ☐ yarn
- ☐ string
- ☐ scraps of fabric, trim, and yarn
- ☐ glue
- ☐ construction paper

HELPFUL HINTS

- Wooden-spoon puppets are appropriate for very young children because they are very easy to use.
- Wooden-spoon puppets make great use of old kitchen spoons.

DEVELOPMENTAL GOALS

Develop creativity and small muscles in fingers and hands, use familiar objects in new ways, and encourage imagination.

PREPARATION

Give each child a wooden spoon.

PROCESS

1. Draw a face on the wooden spoon.
2. Glue yarn or string to the spoon for hair.
3. Glue scraps of fabric and trim to the spoon for clothing.
4. Use and enjoy.

VARIATIONS

- Make real or imaginary wooden-spoon animals.
- Create a family of spoon puppets. Use them in the housekeeping corner.
- Make yourself a spoon puppet.
- Make a new and unique creature that just happens to be a spoon puppet.

NOTES FOR NEXT TIME: ______________________________

____

____

____

Index by Ages

ALL AGES

3 YEARS AND UP

4 YEARS AND UP

5 YEARS AND UP